Antoni Gaudí
Ornament, Fire and Ashes

COLUMNS OF SMOKE / VOL. III

Juan José Lahuerta

Translated by Graham Thomson

TENOV BOOKS

First published in Spanish as *Humaredas. Arquitectura, ornamentación, medios impresos.* Lampreave 2010.

Revised edition published in February 2016

Editorial Tenov
Casp 147
08013 Barcelona
tenov@editorialtenov.com
www.tenovbooks.com

We gratefully acknowledge the invaluable assistance of the Casa Batlló, the Càtedra Gaudí ETSAB UPC, the Col·legi Oficial d'Arquitectes de Catalunya, the Consorci del Patrimoni de Sitges, Escofet, the Fundació Catalunya-La Pedrera, the Fundació Institut Amatller d'Art Hispànic-Arxiu Mas, the Moderna Museet in Stockholm, the Museu Nacional d'Art de Catalunya in Barcelona, Pere Vivas and Triangle Postals.

Design by TENOV and Hector Aspano
Pre-printing l'Estudi, Barcelona
Printed in Norprint, Barcelona

ISBN: 978-84-939231-6-7
DL: B 719-2016

CONTENTS

Nocturne

When so much is suffered without sleep, and the blood
pulses with nothing but the sound of rage,
as your insides shake with wide-awake hatred
and ceaseless vengeance burns in your marrow,
then words are good for nothing: they're words.

Bullets. Bullets.

Manifestos, articles, commentaries, speeches,
lost columns of smoke, printed fog,
what an ache of papers the wind has to sweep up,
what a sadness of ink the water has to wash away!

Bullets. Bullets.

Now I suffer how poor, how mean, how sad,
how wretched and dead a throat
when from the abyss of its language it would
scream what it can't, because impossible, and is dumb.

Bullets. Bullets.

I feel tonight words mortally wounded.

Rafael Alberti,
De un momento a otro (From One Moment to the Next), 1937.
English translation by Graham Thomson

'I PROPOSE TO MAKE A SERIOUS STUDY OF ORNAMENTATION'

In his notes on ornamentation, written in 1878, Gaudí cites a considerable number of historic buildings, but only two from his own time,[1] and it is no accident that these are two great modern Parisian monuments: the new Opéra by Charles Garnier [fig. 3, 5-11], to which he refers twice, begun in 1862, and the Sacré-Cœur by Paul Abadie [fig. 1, 2, 4], whose first stone was placed in 1875, the same year that the Opéra opened. He compares both unfavourably, even slightingly, with great monuments of the past: the Opéra with the Parthenon, and Sacré-Cœur with Gothic cathedrals. Gaudí cannot help but see these buildings, known to him only from photographs and publications, as failed hybrids in which, for all their extraordinary richness and the abundance of materials, the ornamentation has lost its eloquence, its power of conviction: it has literally been uprooted. He qualifies it as 'something that signifies nothing and that no one understands'.[2] His condemnation—Gaudí distrusted a modern architecture in which technique and art seemed to be divorced, in which means did not match ends and the newest structures and materials were masked by a soulless and standardized ornamentation—is typical of the aesthetic moralism of the nineteenth century. And it is on this moralism, rather than on the appropriateness of the language, that the concepts of style and character present in these writings of Gaudí's (thoroughly Violletian, as he admits) are based:[3] writings in which the *decorum* of the ancients, based on shared rules, dissolves into disquisitions on the truth or sincerity of structures, materials and forms and thence into moral judgements as to the legitimacy of personal decisions, those of the architect, whose individualism is nevertheless hailed as his great virtue.

But Gaudí's discourse on ornamentation is more than that. We shall try to follow it to its conclusion, first pausing to consider what he wrote about the Paris Opéra.

fig. 1, 2

fig. 3, 4

Gaudí begins by comparing it to the Parthenon,[4] whose astoundingly rich and beautifully worked materials—marble, ivory, bronze, gold, precious stones...—are not there, he says, to represent wealth or to "cover" the building luxuriously; but constitute its essence: the work, down to the smallest detail, *is made of* these materials, the chief of which, moreover, and the one of which it is actually composed—including the roof tiles—is unique, homogeneous and autochthonous: Pentelic marble. In other words, in the Parthenon there is no difference between material and place, or between material and work, or between material and expression, and still less between material—or ingredient—and matter.

What we find in the Paris Opéra is very different; here the 'marbles from all the world' fail to divert attention from and indeed 'demonstrate the meanness and neglect' with which most of the construction solutions and details have been handled, 'imitating everything and satisfying nothing'. Gaudí is lamenting not so much the lack of correspondence between one part and another and between the parts and the whole—that is, the absence of *concinnitas*, an intellectual quality—but the material disorder of the building, the confusion between the real and the fake, between rich material and tinsel, between the bronze cresting and the vulgar clay tile peeking out from behind it.

On the one hand he complains of the absolute impossibility of distinguishing in this building between what it is and what it could or should be, and that even what it is appears, in the last analysis, as if it were; and on the other, and especially, that the need to create specific moments of great richness has been satisfied only at the expense of the usury practised on the whole. The brimming accumulation of 'sculpture, mouldings, members and yet more exotic members' that occurs on the façade of Garnier's Opéra [fig. 5-11] is presented by Gaudí as a 'mania'. Caprice, extravagance and eccentricity would be some of the synonyms. So, when he writes that this richness, referring only to itself and alien to the whole, achieved at the expense of the impoverishment of the rest, serves only to gratify 'the vanity of the architect', what is he doing but explicitly declaring the moral nature of his judgement? If the architect is vain, so too will his work be: for Gaudí, as for Viollet-le-Duc, this is the essential condition of style and character. As we read a few lines below, the requirement that the architect adjust means to ends is 'a matter of conscience'. There we have, described with severity by Gaudí, the architect who collects elements without satisfying 'any service', without responding to 'any aspiration', with no other end in view than agglomeration for its own sake: sheer quantity is summoned to make amends for impotence, with no understanding,

fig. 5

fig. 6

as Gaudí notes, that quantity raised to the condition of an end in itself simply exposes the essential poverty, since a 'lack of resources' cannot by corrected by quantity alone.

On the basis of this analysis Gaudí takes a significant turn. So far he has referred to the resources of the architect in the sense of his skills; he will now refer to other resources, inseparable from the former: financial resources; though of course he is talking not about the *lack* of these resources, but the opposite: the Paris Opéra has suffered from no shortage of means and yet the result is petty. What is the reason for this paradox? Gaudí states it clearly: 'all the treasures of Napoleon III' are to no avail from the moment that 'the constructions have taken a separate path from the decoration, and this has gone counter to them.'

Let's look at the order of this phrase of Gaudí's, or rather, at its symmetry. Between construction and decoration Gaudí does not establish any hierarchy. It is not the decoration that has uprooted the construction, as established in due course by the orthodox process of modernity, which starts out thinking of decoration as superfluous and ends up condemning it as a 'crime',[5] while at the same time assigning to the construction the role of conserving the essential qualities of the useful and the true. On the contrary, in Gaudí's proposition construction and decoration are situated on the same level and have the same value, and it could even be said, on the basis of the first part of his premise, that it was construction that initiated this distancing between the two. Construction is inhibited and at the same time, as a result of this, decoration loses its footing: in short, construction and decoration become estranged from one another.

But what, then, is the reason for this opposition, this reciprocal expulsion? At this point, Gaudí's critique definitely separates itself from—if it had ever had anything to do with—considerations of aesthetics or 'taste', and appeals to an ultimate, 'logical' motive above and beyond the simple, because obvious, confrontation between construction and decoration: the real conflict, in fact, is between architecture and reality.

'The commitment,' Gaudí writes, 'must be not only to undertaking grand projects, but to making them realizable.' Gaudí is speaking, therefore, of a question of possibilities; to put it bluntly, of economics: 'make projects economically feasible and as a result embrace the conditions of production of our time.' It is not, then, a question of a greater or lesser amount of material and financial resources, let

following pages fig. 7, 8

alone of the 'excess' of those resources, but of the appropriate 'use' that is or is not made of them. For Gaudí, the ultimate rationale of all synthesis lies in the correspondence between the project and its 'conditions of production', and only through that correspondence will architecture speak in a true language.

The issue of use, of economics, runs all the way through these notes by Gaudí on ornament, as the principal reflection, as it does in his report on his project for streetlights for the streets and squares of Barcelona, also from 1878, and his review—the only text he was to see published—of the Exhibition of Decorative Arts in 1881.[6]

In the comparison he makes between the Gothic cathedrals and the Sacré-Cœur the same issue is once again the main argument. On the one hand, he says, the works of his time can no longer compete with the great mediaeval cathedrals, in that while the latter are the expression of a collective religiosity, the former are the expression of a fetishistic cult of what can no longer be achieved. In the 'continuation of the Gothic styles' he sees, in effect, not a true aspiration to the Divine but the 'adoration' of the Middle Ages; that is to say, of art and of history. Art, and more particularly the mythicised art of the Middle Ages, has become an end in itself and the greatest of tyrannies. 'Religious objects are slaves of a profane idea: art,' he tells us, and goes on to insist that we find ourselves in a situation in which the 'logic' between means and ends has been reversed: art no longer 'identifies itself with religion in order to express it, as it should be' but 'imposes itself as a style', as 'a pretext for serving up a purely plastic form' with the result that 'we necessarily produce incomplete buildings, which say nothing.'[7]

At the time of the triumph of *l'art pour l'art*, of the bohemian invention of the religion of art—and we shall discuss this subject in the next chapter—Gaudí was lamenting the lack of eloquence of modern architecture and attributing it precisely to its having lost contact with the things that are real and true, which are, ultimately, *beyond* art and beyond the 'purely plastic'.

However, this loss has not occurred only in relation to the transcendent.

Once again, Gaudí's discourse contains an inflection that situates it directly in the most material reality. If we produce 'incomplete buildings' it is because '*moreover* [emphasis added], the means of execution have changed completely'. The question of the 'conditions of production of our time' thus reappears in all its rawness, and as the main argument.

LE NOUVEL OPÉRA DE PARIS

SCULPTURE ORNEMENTALE

DUCHER et Cie, Editeurs.
Durandelle, Photographe.

LE NOUVEL OPÉRA
DE PARIS

Echelle de 0m03 pr mètre

Bernard del. CHARLES GARNIER, ARCHte J. Penel sc.

DÉTAIL DE LA FAÇADE PRINCIPALE

DUCHER et Cie, Editeurs. Imp. Ch. et A. Chardon _ Paris.

Indeed, Gaudí could not be more of a realist: in the Middle Ages, he says, 'all of the idealized filigree of those temples could be done because the cost was not excessive. Today, the smallest sculpture [...] costs the earth; the higher price of labour makes it impossible to be lavish with mouldings, fretwork, etcetera, or profuse with sculpture; and *therefore* [emphasis added] we have to be frugal and even mean'.

That 'moreover' and that 'therefore' close a circle that overlaps the other circle that seeks to supply transcendental reasons for the meannesses of this architecture: reasons based on aristocratic questions of 'taste' or on aesthetico-moral judgements. These judgements and these questions make up the background of commonplaces to Gaudí's text, but the real crux of his discourse stands out quite crudely against this background: namely, the economy.

Let's consider this reflection on the very high quality of the mediaeval craftsman linked to low cost of his product, immediately contrasted with the poverty of contemporary production, combined, conversely, with its high price. What is Gaudí doing here but making the hardships and the meanness of modern decoration the quintessential image of the impotence of the construction of his age? Undoubtedly he is, but does he in passing manifest any nostalgia for the great skill of the mediaeval craftsmen? Not a trace. In Gaudí's discourse there is admiration, but no nostalgia. There is also, and above all from the point where he crudely highlights economic considerations, cost and price as inextricably bound up with quality, an explicit recognition that quality no longer exists or can exist: that the past is gone. For Gaudí, as we have seen, the first lesson to be drawn from the past is the appropriate 'use' of 'the conditions of production', and this has no place for either mythicising or nostalgia.

We now have a better understanding of Gaudí's critique of his era's idolatry of the mediaeval. Had not the Middle Ages been presented precisely as a time when the craftsman reigned supreme? And is not the craft utopia a redemptionist utopia? The sublimation of craft is neither more nor less than the dream of work liberated from the conditions of production, whose quality lies above and beyond 'use' and 'the useful'. In marked contrast, at the time of writing these notes, in 1878, Gaudí believed not in ideal relations of production, but only in 'the conditions of production of our time'. That was his realism: to clearly affirm that we neither can nor should look for the redemptive return of the mediaeval craftsman, and that utopian longing cannot pass itself off as the expression of the poetic freedom of the architect without compromising the 'possibilities' of architecture.

Let's move on to the review of the Exhibition of Decorative Arts in Barcelona, which Gaudí published in 1881.[8] He praises, albeit in a rather passionless way, the 'good execution' of most of the exhibits, but is sharply critical of the vulgarity of their forms and the dearth of ideas—'imitations of antiquated French industry abound'[9]—and what in today's terms would be called a lack of design. This modern claiming of a role in the initial stage of the process of producing objects—the necessity of an 'idea', of 'design' and, in short, of an architect—is accompanied by a considerable didactic effort, whose main aim is to demonstrate that a product of genuine quality is achieved not by an excess of means, but by the proper use of however few means may be available.

Gaudí laments the fact that the teaching of design focuses 'more on the handling of the pencil and the formation of general taste than of industrial taste, which must be more concrete than the former'. But what does 'concrete' mean in this context? Once again, the meaning of things is conceived in relation to the means of production: the study of good models from the past and present ought to enable us, Gaudí says, to recognize 'the working conditions in which they were executed'. Only then will the industrialist appreciate that 'it is not through the accumulation of labour [...] that good products are made, but by giving the proper form to the use and the materials, and much of the time simply applying the means of execution'.[10]

Appropriate use, then, of the available means. It is not surprising that Gaudí's whole article is based, as he explicitly says, on drawing comparisons between the generally modest quality of the new products and the 'evident [...] superiority' of the objects exhibited in the antiques section.

But let's look at how this superiority is demonstrated in a particular case. Gaudí is describing the beautiful ornamentation of a little antique box of carved cypress wood, whose working is so simple that 'an apprentice would be able to do it'.[11] That is the key: the design is adapted to its means and its ends in such a way as to determine the execution and render unnecessary the intervention of that great mythical craftsman and absurd any aspiration to the Protean craftsman, who exists only in the most idealized production relations.

The championing of a 'concrete' industrial taste becomes, for Gaudí, both the solution and the programme. Indeed, the 1881 article can be treated as an effective didactic application of the notes of 1878, although in truth, rather than focusing on a discussion of an industrial aesthetic, as a question of taste *tout court*, the major part of Gaudí's discourse is concerned, as we have seen, with economics. So it is not surprising that his notes should deal above all with ornamentation—for which there is no entry in Viollet-le-Duc's *Dictionnaire Raisonné*[12]—and that he should start by stating that their purpose is to make it 'interesting and intelligible'.[13] Ornamentation is the point at which Gaudí sees the possibility of art and industry coming together, and sees that possibility, far from being mythical, as being logical, given that the quality of the ornamentation, and consequently, the potential eloquence of the architecture, cannot be abstracted from the resources and costs of its production.

Let us return, then, to the 1878 notebook. 'At present, everything that tends to elevate the labour tends to lower the value of the materials.'[14] With this statement, somewhat confusing though it is, located in the core of his text, Gaudí commences a lengthy paragraph that is entirely economic in content. The sentence quoted here is glossed in the following lines, which explain how the result of the 'application of machines that produce great quantities in a short time' has been the extraordinary increase in the price of skilled labour, linked to the scarcity of high quality one-off products. But here once again the reflection is not nostalgic; on the contrary, it concludes in a eulogy to the potential of industry. Gaudí writes enthusiastically of all that the age places at his disposal, from 'powerful machines for crushing stone' to 'steam traction engines' and from 'hydrolyzed limes' to industries that 'have emerged in the last few years': painted glass, metal foundries, machines for sawing marble, tile factories and so on.

'Let us not spend fruitlessly on things that mean nothing but rather attend to the essentials, morally and materially,' Gaudí writes. The example of that antique carved box he refers to in his article of 1881, which we recalled above, where a mere apprentice, for all his limitations, can achieve exceptionally high quality if its execution is applied to actual material resources and economic possibilities, ties in perfectly with these ideas, and constitutes a radical denunciation of any craft utopia as an outdated illusion.

Gaudí speaks in terms of a real industrial pedagogy: it is a question of forming the taste of both the public and the producers, starting by making them aware of what the 'conditions of production of our time' are in an age when the unique, one-off production of the old craftsman has become economically and socially unattainable.

Nº 38
75

LE NOUVEL OPERA
DE PARIS
DÉTAIL DE LA FAÇADE PRINCIPALE

fig. 9, 10, 11

The artisans of the mediaeval cathedrals were artists inspired by the Divine; contemporary art, however, invokes nothing beyond itself, and through the strategy of *l'art pour l'art* has placed itself at the summit of the luxury market, rendering impossible its *application* in architectural decoration, so that the only possible, realistic *application* is that of the modern, industrial means: surely this is what Gaudí is saying?

In 1878 Gaudí understood very well that architecture could no longer count on the unique work of great artists; his industrial pedagogy revolves around a realistic question: how to organize production. Clearly, Gaudí was saying no to that mythicised craftsmanship, and also to the banality of standardized mass production, as he makes clear in his article of 1881, and declaring himself in favour of quality industrial manufacturing.

If we bear in mind this Gaudí who so consciously opposes the craft utopia and no less consciously extols the possibilities of industrial production when we contemplate the totality of his work, which had yet to be initiated in 1878, do we not seem to be faced with a paradox? Perhaps so, but in any case this paradox does not exist if we analyse the mechanisms of ornamental production of his first commissions.

I refer the reader at this point to a couple of earlier texts in which I sought to relate the mechanisms of composition Gaudí used in his first constructions, based on juxtaposition, collage and parataxis, with the way in which these notes on ornamentation are composed.[15] At the same time it would not be inappropriate, in considering these modes of composition, to remark the similarity between the graphic layout of the pages of some of the most popular treatises on ornamentation of the time, such as *The Grammar of Ornament* by Owen Jones, and Gaudí's first works [fig. 12-18, 39-43].[16] In Jones's treatise, and especially in the sections entitled 'Arabian Ornament', without doubt the most likely to have interested Gaudí at this early stage of his career, the plates are arranged around a larger central motive—square in Arabian No. 2 [fig. 14], circular in Arabian No. 3 [fig. 16]—surrounded by smaller rectangular motives, each in its own cell, with the intricate patterns of the arabesques or tracery cut short by the edges but at the same time compensated by the other motives in a kind of suggested or *sickly* symmetry (we vaguely intuit a socle, a wider central body, lateral elements reminiscent of pilasters...), the whole topped with rows of crenellated battlements.

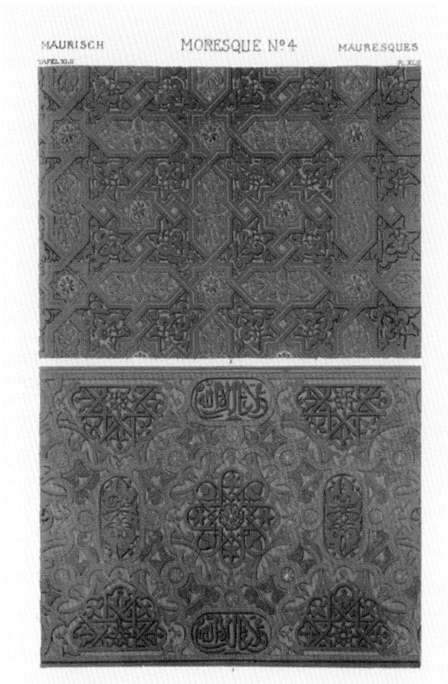

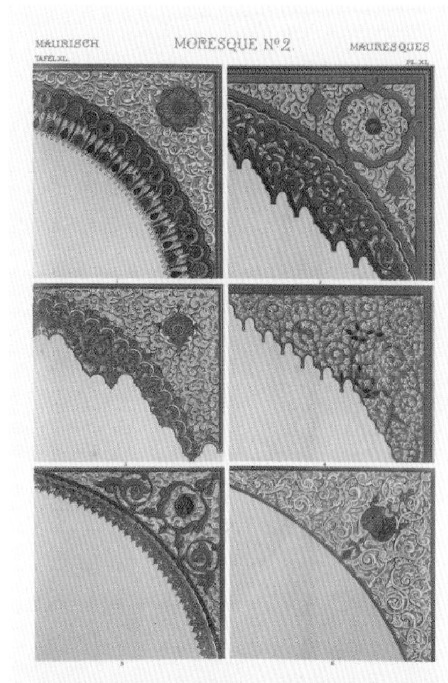

fig. 12, 13, 14, 15

fig. 16

fig. 17

fig. 18

We need only observe Gaudí's earliest works—notably the stables he built for Eusebi Güell, with their ornamentals sections cut off and framed by brickwork, juxtaposed with a vague sense of the tectonic and also topped with battlements—to perceive the similarity [fig. 17-18, 39-43]. It was not just the ornamental motives in Owen Jones, then, that interested Gaudí, but also the composition; or rather, the combination of these motives in systems framed and juxtaposed in such a way that a graphic resource, inspired by architectural composition, returns to the architectural realm in an exchange that surely calls for more attention.

But we shall focus now on other issues. Firstly, on the way in which, in these early works, especially El Capricho [fig. 21, 22] and, still more, the Vicens house [fig. 24, 25], both begun around 1883, the rhetorical development of the structure is smoothly and seamlessly converted into ornamental expression. In the body of the construction, the courses of stone and tiles create a horizontal cadence that contrasts in El Capricho with the verticality of the cornice brackets and, much more violently, in the Vicens house, with the exaggerated vertical rhythm of the gallery and the even more intense and compressed rhythm of the partitions of the roof (in fact a monumental interpretation of the traditional Catalan flat roof structure), projected outward as towering gables raised on narrow corbels. Structure, geometry and rhythm: here, on an equal footing and thanks to a great 'will to style', construction and ornament come together. But there is more. In both cases, Gaudí used the tiles to culminate this ornamental process, and in both cases the enormously rich effect of variety, movement and colour is obtained from a very small number of pieces designed by the architect himself, inspired, no doubt, by British models [fig. 19, 20]: two in El Capricho and just one in the Vicens house.

In El Capricho these are embossed glazed pieces [fig. 23]: one represents the head of a sunflower, the other its leaf, and it is the way these are combined that allows all of the effects. Here again, though, the Vicens house is the more interesting case. There Gaudí designed, as I said, a single piece: a smooth tile decorated with three flowers, two buds and some leaves of the French marigold, capable of combination in all directions, to create densely matted surfaces of flowery fields [fig. 26]. But this is not the only tile used on the Vicens façade: there are two others, one white and one green, standard plain tiles which sometimes combine with one another and sometimes with the marigold tile to form checkerboards, but are used above all to intensify to a maddening degree the rhythmic effect of the cantilevered partitions of the crown [fig. 25].

fig. 19, 20

fig. 21, 22, 23

A. T. V. — 2013 - BARCELONA, Construcciones modernas
Calle de S. Gervasio, num. 24
Arquitecto : Antonio Gaudi

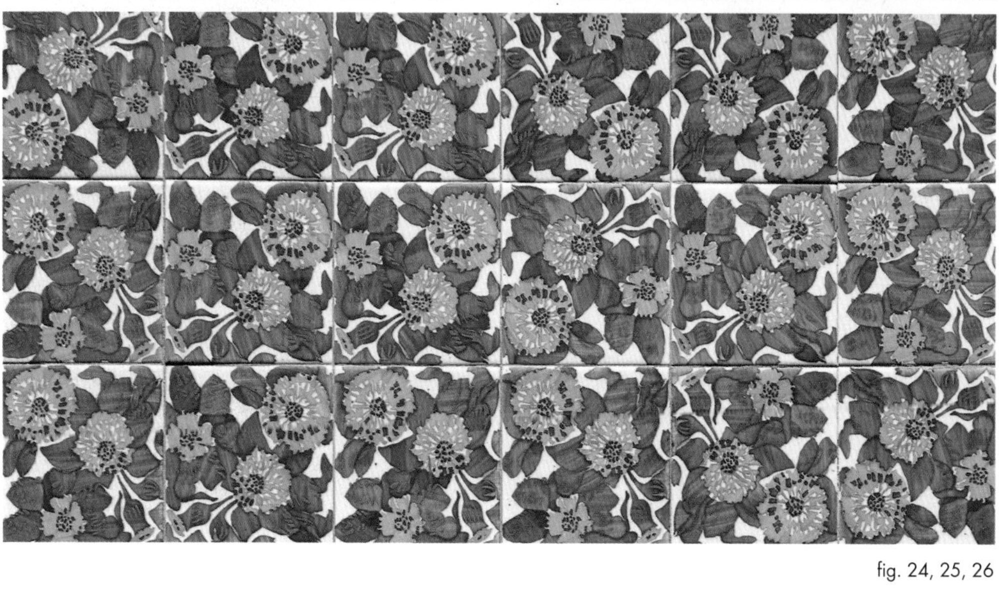

fig. 24, 25, 26

fig. 27

fig. 28, 29

In connection with his ideas on the logic of ornament, expressed in the text of 1878, this use of tiles is exemplary: industrially produced elements and a radical reduction of the number of pieces (two, three) to achieve the largest and most varied effects. What is Gaudí doing here but applying and demonstrating the effectiveness of those ideas about the proper use of the means of production? Is he not attaining, through the most appropriate and economical exploitation of the resources offered by industrial production, the high quality ornamentation and the power of eloquence that will enable him to scotch the myth of the good craftsman?

The fact is there was no need for a great artist or even a great craftsman to model that sunflower or those leaves, or to draw those marigolds, which were then produced in series and which already contained, precisely in their industrial form, the mechanisms of their combination: nevertheless, the final effect was to be truly admirable.

But there is, in the Vicens house, another element from which we can draw further lessons: the famous railing, traditionally vaunted by historians as one of the highlights of Gaudí's craftsmanship [fig. 27]. But let's look more closely at how it is made. The main piece is of cast iron, a highly realistic representation of a palmetto leaf, its lacinias resting on a ring, which is bolted in its turn to the rectangles of the mesh that forms the real structure of the railing, made up of industrially milled L-shaped bars; at the intersections of these bars is a fleuron, also of cast iron, in the form of a marigold bud [fig. 28, 29].

To construct his railing, then, Gaudí used just three elements, one of which, the L-shaped bar, is a standard industrial product; the other two are cast: that is to say, serially produced from a mould. Metalsmithing, a technique in which the artisan's skill can clearly be appreciated, and a technique that in the final years of the nineteenth century came to constitute one of the great myths of the 'mediaevalist' craft revival in Catalonia, is reduced in this work to an entirely secondary motive—the spikes that top the railing—while the cast pieces, whose serial character was much criticised at the time, and unfavourably compared to metalsmithing and its manual qualities, are elevated here to the lead role. Not only that, but instead of being modelled by a sculptor, as it ought to have been, the palmetto leaf was cast from a mould of a real specimen: hence its realism. In other words, Gaudí was giving first place to what sculptors called *ars infamis*: not an imitation of nature but merely a mould taken from nature, by simple contact, stealing nature's forms.[17]

Here again, then, what we have is not artistic modelling but a mechanical process, casting, as a means of dispensing with the 'good craftsman'. It is not just that the great artist no longer exists or is economically unaffordable, but that, as we well know, the 'good craftsman' is a utopia. We should note here, by the way, that Gaudí knew the limitations of his craftsmen: he entrusted the casting of the palmetto to the sculptor Llorenç Matamala, who years later was to take charge of the sculpture of the Sagrada Família, and was succeeded in this task by his son. Thus, in the notes on ornamentation, we read: 'M. has become an idler and less than active [...]. What is needed is the counterweight: method, method and method [...]'.[18] As Laura Mercader has said, the 'M' here probably stands for Matamala. If those mythical artisans had passed away for good, then instead of lamenting, what could be better than to fill their place with the means afforded by 'the conditions of production of our time'? Serial casting and industrial pressed parts were among those conditions, together with moulds taken from nature.

The palmetto, the single, dominant motive, with its great concavity, with the recessing of the well-separated points of its lacinias, has in itself a marked plastic quality, impressive both for the chiaroscuro it creates in the interior and for its nuanced transparency. By the simple process of repeating it in long horizontal bands, with the tips of the leaves alternately pointing inwards and outwards, Gaudí achieves an exceptional surface that vibrates with the light with the same intensity and the same infinite nuances as a field of palmettos stirred by the wind. Once again, then, we find Gaudí obtaining the most striking results with the minimal resources offered by the repetition of a standard or serially produced industrial component. Between 1878 and the middle of the eighteen eighties, what better implementation could there be of his reflections on economic logic as the source and guarantor of the true value of ornament?

It may not be amiss to take a look here, in order to confirm this attitude and this way of working, at another great work of the same period, mentioned above: the carriage entrance to the estate of Eusebi Güell in Pedralbes, with its very wide single-leaf gate in the form of a gigantic dragon, made in or around 1885 [fig. 30, 39-43].

The lower part is a rectangular diagonal grille five metres long, consisting of two great parallel industrial H-beams with different sections joined by a diagonal mesh of lighter T-section bars, welded to the diamond-shaped gaps occupied by little square cast iron plates with the relief of a rose inscribed in a circular concavity [fig. 34].

fig. 30

fig. 31, 32, 33, 34, 35

Here again, then, the minimal combination of industrial parts and a single serial motive is capable of creating at one and the same time and without conflict the structure and the rhythm of the construction and the ornament, a repetitive structure and rhythm that are evidently inherent in the conditions of their industrial production.

On top of this diagonal grille sits the famous dragon, one of the most important sculptures of Gaudí's whole career. We should bear in mind that it was originally polychrome, with red jaws, with glass balls shining in its now empty eye sockets, and that a latch mechanism moved its front talon when the door was opened or closed [fig. 30, 32].

However, this awesome dragon is more than just a sculpture. For a start it is an essential part of the structure of the gate, serving as it does as the tie needed to hold up such a wide and heavy gate leaf: in fact, the digits of its wings perform this mechanical function. But there is another question that is of even more interest to us. If this carriage gate had been composed from a traditional point of view, the dragon, as the sculptural crown or finish of the piece, would have been resolved in genuinely 'sculptural' terms: it would have been modelled in a more or less naturalistic way and then in all probability executed in wrought iron or cast iron. Gaudí's sculpture, in contrast, is the product of assembling a series of components whose origins, once again, are industrial: the dragon's long spiralling tail is a spring [fig. 35], the membrane of its wings is very fine wire mesh [fig. 33], the chains and bars are prefabricated [fig. 31, 34], and the scales of the beast's legs and body, its jaws and fangs, its snout, its eyes and its spines ... are of sheet metal [fig. 32].

Prefabricated pieces, sheet metal and welding: clearly neither the materials nor the techniques call for the exceptional skills of the mythical artisan, but can be worked perfectly well in the industrial metal shop. When we contemplate the dragon from a distance we have the impression of a highly complex sculpture, rich in detail and virtuoso execution, of considerable volume. As we approach it, however, we are struck by the deliberate brutalism in the choice of materials and their working and, above all, by the fact that except for the head that projects out from the gate, this dragon, which has a very important mechanical function to perform, is flat.

This dragon could have been a giant piece of chinoiserie, but instead it was resolved in the most modern way possible: a modernity that Gaudí understood as a question of possibilities, as the realistic use of the 'conditions of production of our time'. When we look at that head [fig. 32], with its cut and welded metal plates, we could hardly be further from any sense that we are contemplating one of those over-elaborate pieces of ornamental forging or casting of that era and instead, with very little effort of the imagination, something very different and intimately familiar: should it be any surprise that the greatest of the historic avant-garde artists in iron sculpture, Juli González (1876-1942), executed his best works in cut and welded sheet metal? Born in Barcelona, into a family of goldsmiths, he began his career in the heyday of Modernisme and was employed for a while in Gaudí's Sagrada Família workshop: would he not have spent more time contemplating that dragon, among other 'industrial' works by Gaudí, than has been supposed? And was it not thanks to González that artists like Gargallo (1881-1934) and Picasso (1881-1972), both by no means coincidentally formed in the same artistic milieu of Barcelona Modernisme, came to use the same industrial technique in their sculptures?

But let's leave these digressions, however fruitful they may be, and return to Gaudí. His dragon is also, then, the dragon of the world of industry, of the Evil of modernity, of the factories, of the city, opposed by the Garden of the Hesperides, the Villa Satalia—those were the names of Eusebi Güell's estate—as the family home converted into the pure and perfectly isolated *hortus conclusus* guarded by a now domesticated dragon.

Gaudí's work in these early commissions for rural locations (El Capricho, the Vicens house, the Güell estate...), in which his ideas on the means of ornamentation of a few years earlier seem to be embodied to perfection, is joyful and ironic.

One cannot help but think, once again, of the Vicens house, with the ivy climbing the walls of its interior rooms, which are covered, too, with reeds or ferns, and on the painted ceramic tiles of whose socles we find varieties of marigold, the same flowers blooming in the garden around the house and on the tiles of its façades, while painted bushes, branches and bunches of cherries cluster between the rafters on the plaster of the ceiling [fig. 36]. And there is more: papier-mâché birds circle above the fireplace, moved by the warm air [fig. 38]; the sash windows, on being opened or closed, emit music reminiscent of birdsong; the water of the fountain in the glazed balcony flows over a metal spider's web in a fine layer that refracts the sunlight into the colours of the rainbow [fig. 37] ... and finally, as we know, the iron railing repeats a palmetto leaf cast from one of those growing on the site when the work commenced, among many other surprises.

fig. 36, 37, 38

fig. 39

fig. 40

A. T. V. — 140 - BARCELONA
Puerta de la casa de campo
de D. Eusebio Güell

fig. 41, 42, 43

sont sculptés avec une verve et un entrain remarquables (fig. 12). On voit d'assez beaux fleurons à la cathédrale d'Amiens, autour de celle de Paris, à Saint-Ouen de Rouen, à Saint-Étienne d'Auxerre, à la cathé-

11

drale de Clermont, à Saint-Just de Narbonne et à Saint-Nazaire de Carcassonne ; mais le grand défaut de la sculpture du XIVe siècle, c'est le manque de variété, et ce défaut est particulièrement choquant lorsqu'il s'agit de couronnements qui se voient tous à peu près dans les mêmes conditions.

Au XVe siècle, les fleurons qui terminent les pinacles ou les gâbles

particulièrement l'*Arum* et l'*Iris ;* ces deux plantes donnent, dès le commencement du XIIe siècle, une physionomie particulière à l'orne-

10

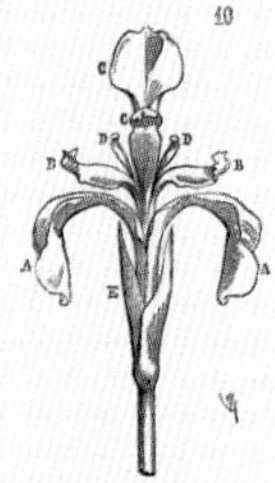

11

mentation sculptée ou peinte (voy. PEINTURE). Quelle était la raison qui

12

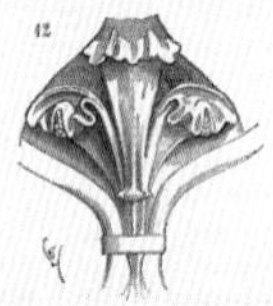

13

avait fait choisir de préférence ces végétaux des lieux humides, qui arrivent à leur floraison dès les premiers jours du printemps? M. Woillez,

de Fougère dont nous avons donné plus haut quelques brins ? et ces

3

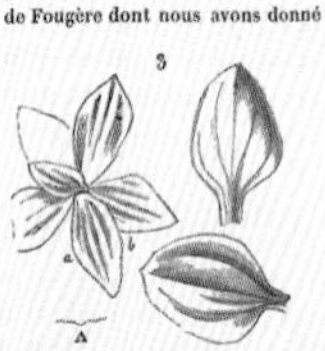

3 *bis*

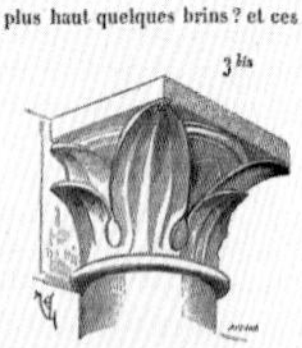

feuilles naissantes de Plantain (fig. 3) n'ont-elles pas inspiré les artistes

4

qui sculptaient les chapiteaux du chœur de l'église de Vézelay, ceux de la galerie du chœur de Notre-Dame de Paris (fig. 3 *bis*), ou ceux de l'église de Montréal (Yonne) (fig. 4)? N'y a-t-il pas, entre les petites

système de construction (voy. CATHÉDRALE, CONSTRUCTION), comme

2

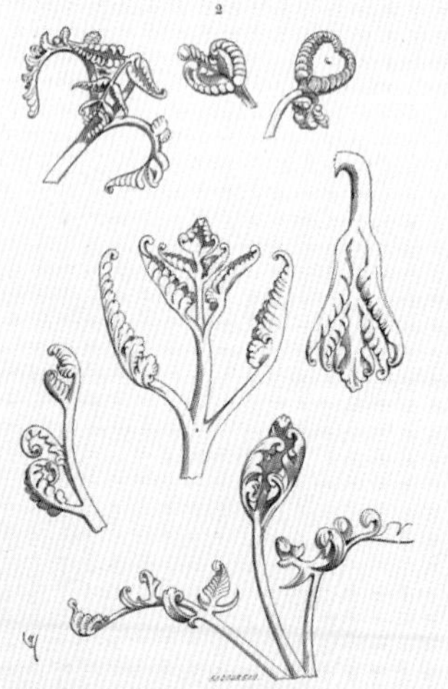

méthode de bâtir, les architectes laïques de la seconde moitié du

fig. 44

BLATTER NACH DER NATUR
LEAVES FROM NATURE, Nº 9
FEUILLES D'APRES NATURE
TAFEL XCIX.
PL. XCIX

fig. 45

The plants and flowers that Gaudí found on the plot when he visited it for the first time are the motives constituting the house's ornamentation, both exterior and interior, and in this our architect was interpreting, literally and with great good humour, something that Viollet-le-Duc says in the entry on 'Flora' in the *Dictionnaire Raisonné*, namely that the work of the mediaeval sculptor was inspired not by standardized Roman traditions or Byzantine abstract geometric patterns but by picking from the ground a fern leaf, examining it with curiosity and, passionately excited by so beautiful a creation of nature, carving his capital [fig. 44].[19] Ruskin too speaks in *The Bible of Amiens* of 'those fruits, those flowers, those leaves and those branches' that the sculptors of the cathedral took from the vegetation of the surrounding area and, as Proust stresses, went on to carve 'in Amiens wood'.[20]

Instead of Doric or Ionic geometric mouldings and scrolls, instead of the standardized Corinthian acanthus, the fine leaf of the fern, or of 'parsley, cabbage, lettuce, cauliflower, celery ...',[21] all those market garden vegetables that Gaudí recalls in his notes of 1878 as forming part, as opposed to the standardized acanthus, of the repertoire of 'innumerable' Gothic capitals, 'now that the study of vegetation and botany has rendered vulgar plants that have great conditions of ornamentation';[22] and now, we might add, following on from Gaudí's reflections, that industrial techniques and the 'conditions of production of our time' allow their profusion. Indeed, the whole final chapter of the treatise by Owen Jones that we mentioned before is devoted—and for the same reasons—to 'Leaves and Flowers from Nature' [fig. 45]. The work of that mediaeval sculptor who lovingly collected fern leaves can therefore be matched in quality, although, far from any nostalgia, it will have very different, 'contemporary' shades, and will be achieved by very different means.

It seems clear, then, that Gaudí's intentions in those first works, begun in 1883-84, shortly after the writing of the texts, correspond with them, but did he hold to these criteria throughout the rest of his career? There is no doubt that Gaudí came increasingly to champion craft work, and that he raised traditional techniques such as wrought iron to a pitch of perfection and virtuosity it would be hard to match. But it is equally true that he never stopped using industrial or serially produced materials, and never lost his taste for the kind of brutalist execution we have seen in the dragon on the Güell estate, which in its way is inseparable from the idea of industrial production, although over time his intentions were inflected and ideologically charged by a more transcendent interpretation of the world as original matter or clay. fig. 46

HERMOSA Y SOLEMNE FIESTA EN LA COLONIA GÜELL

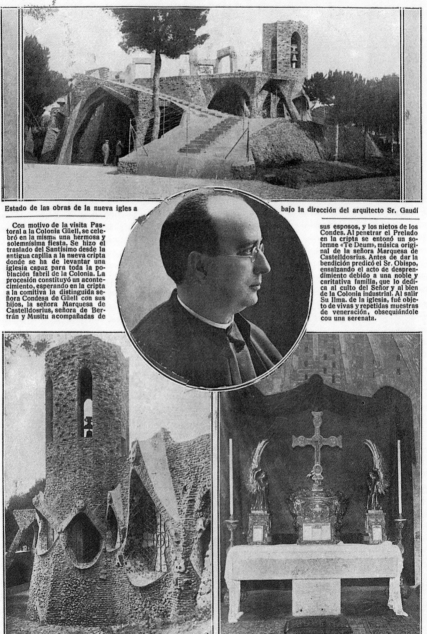

Estado de las obras de la nueva igles a bajo la dirección del arquitecto Sr. Gaudí

Con motivo de la visita Pastoral a la Colonia Güell, se celebró en la misma una hermosa y solemnísima fiesta. Se hizo el traslado del Santísimo desde la antigua capilla a la nueva cripta donde se ha de levantar una iglesia capaz para toda la población fabril de la Colonia. La procesión constituyó un acontecimiento, esperando en la cripta a la comitiva la distinguida señora Condesa de Güell con sus hijos, la señora Marquesa de Castelldosrius, señora de Bertrán y Musitu acompañadas de sus esposos, y los nietos de los Condes. Al penetrar el Prelado en la cripta se entonó un solemne «Te Deum», música original de la señora Marquesa de Castelldosrius. Antes de dar la bendición predicó el Sr. Obispo, ensalzando el acto de desprendimiento debido a una noble y caritativa familia, que lo dedica al culto del Señor y al bien de la Colonia industrial. Al salir Su Ilma. de la iglesia, fué objeto de vivas y repetidas muestras de veneración, obsequiándole cou una serenata.

Un detalle de la iglesia El Sr. Obispo despues de inaugurarl a cripta.—(Fts. B. y C.) Altar mayor de la cripta

fig. 47, 48

fig. 49, 50, 51

fig. 52, 53

FÓTOS DE LES AUS QUE SERVIREN PERA MODELAR ELS FRISOS DE LA FAÇANA DEL NAIXEMENT

fig. 54, 55

What are we to think, for example, when we look at that culminating work, the Crypt for the Colònia Güell, begun in 1908 [fig. 46, 47]? On the one hand, it uses waste materials: burnt bricks, undressed stone, broken tiles [fig. 48], needles scavenged from the dismantling of the old spinning machines from the adjacent factory [fig. 49]; on the other, these materials are deployed almost unworked and untreated, with a deliberate clumsiness, in a violent collage: leaning pillars, monolithic columns of basalt and lead, domed vaults, ribs running in all directions, labyrinthine layouts [fig. 50, 51]... It would not be difficult to find in all of this a distant memory of those ideas about making use of the existing 'conditions of production', but the interpretation has ceased to be humorous and has now become tragic.

But the truth is that all through Gaudí's career the most visible techniques derive from that initial economic interpretation of the ornament. Can the massive use of photography and of casting from moulds taken from nature—two techniques that embody the *ars infamis*— in the gigantic sculptural enterprise of the Sagrada Família [fig. 52-55] be due to anything other than Gaudí's recognition of the technical and artistic limitations of his sculptors and the impossibility of paying the higher wages—and indulging the caprices—of more skilled personnel? Is not *trencadís* [fig. 48, 114] the practice of cladding a surface with broken pieces of ceramic and utilizing an inexpensive method based on the recovery of otherwise unusable waste materials, which does not require specialist skills, a means of avoiding a highly specialized craft technique such as mosaic? And is it not, finally, by means of such possibilist substitutions that Gaudí obtains his most modern—that is to say, 'contemporary'—most wonderful and most sublime results?

And now just one more example, if perhaps the most eloquent, of the extent of Gaudí's understanding of industrial processes. From the end of the nineteenth century, a new type of industrial flooring, cheaper than marble, much easier to work than stoneware and much easier to preserve than wood, became increasingly popular in the construction of bourgeois Barcelona: the mosaic of square hydraulic cement tiles, usually measuring 15 or 20 centimetres to a side. If we look at the magnificent product catalogue published in 1900 by the firm of Escofet & Cia., the leading manufacturers of these cement tiles, we find that the great architects of Modernisme, such as Domènech i Montaner [fig. 57, 58] and Puig i Cadafalch [fig. 56], worked on their designs. We need only visit the houses of Barcelona's Eixample to admire these floors, which follow the rectangular form of the room: the centre is laid to give the appearance of large densely patterned

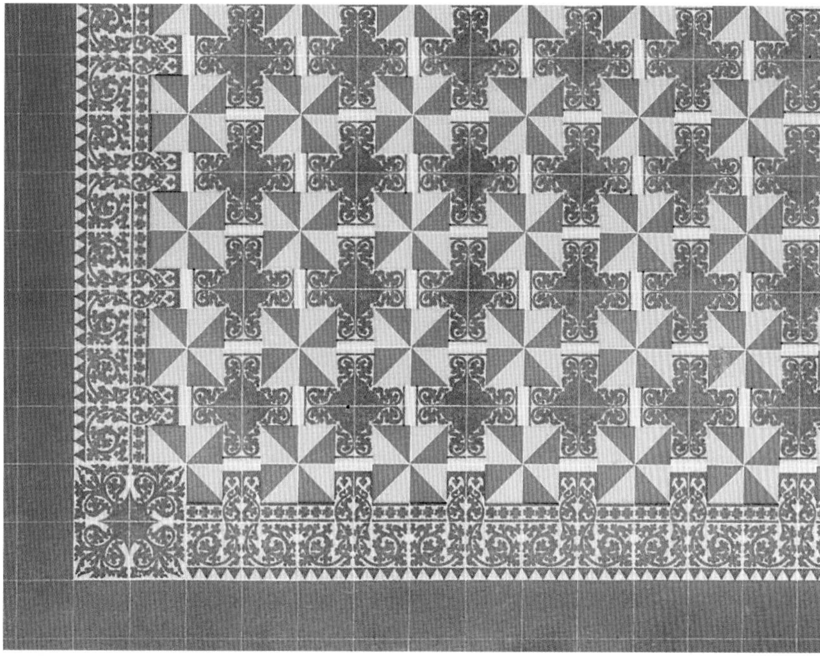

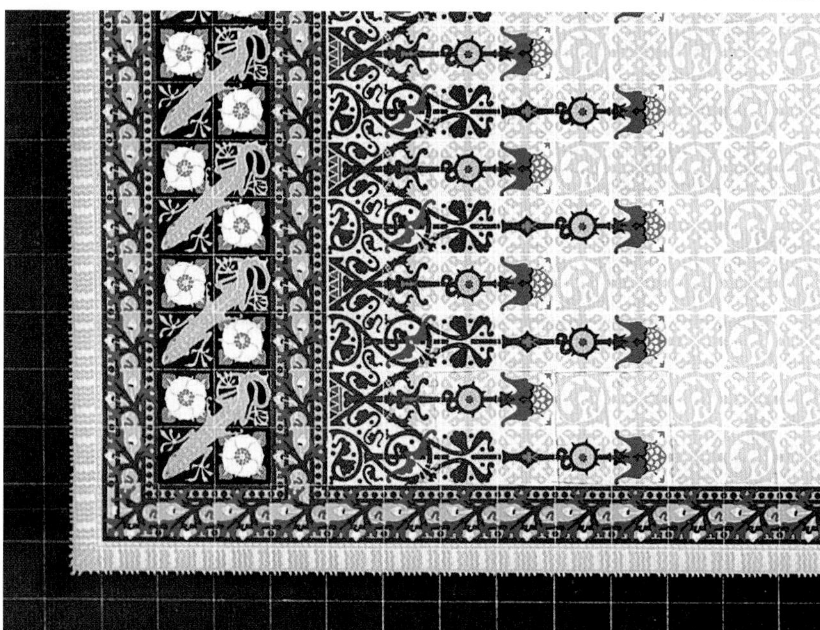

fig. 56, 57

colouristic carpets with the most varied motives, surrounded by several decorative borders and usually terminating at the periphery with monochrome bands, easier to adapt to any irregularities in the walls. In the case of the more elaborate designs, the floor of a single room may require between 20 and 25 different tiles [fig. 58]. Now, the cement tile floor that Gaudí designed for the Batlló house he built on Barcelona's Passeig de Gràcia between 1904 and 1907—which we shall consider at some length in the next chapter—and finally used in the Milà house, begun in 1906 just a few blocks further up the same street, is composed of a single hexagonal monochrome tile [fig. 59-61, 63]. Measuring 15 centimetres to a side, this tile is patterned in relief with one third of each of three marine motives: an ammonite, a starfish and seaweed. It would not be irrelevant to recall here that Ernst Haeckel had serially published the prints of his *Kunstformen der Natur* between 1899 and 1904 [fig. 62, 64], when he brought them together in a single volume essentially devoted to marine creatures, among the most important being precisely the radiolaria, ammonites and jellyfish;[23] these forms, all based on the spiral or vortex, are composed by the combination of the tiles, which creates an intricate surface, at once richly varied and homogeneous, vibrantly alive, without recognizable axes or jointing, and wholly independently of the shape of the room, rectangular or not; and, in fact, the rooms of the Milà and Batlló houses are anything but rectangular.

So in contrast to the varied repertoire of colours and designs, and the number of different pieces his colleagues needed to get their ornamental floors, almost always at odds with the irregularities of the walls, Gaudí reduces everything to a single component that transcends all of these conflicts, adapts to every set of circumstances, and achieves the greatest formal effects.

At the culminating moment of Gaudí's career, then, when he was considered the greatest of eccentrics—the architect who most thoroughly embodied the type of the bohemian artist and, turning market relations on their head, no longer sought to satisfy the needs and desires of his clients or even to work for his public but to impose his own canons of taste—we find him using the most minimal means to achieve the greatest effects, in an exercise based entirely on industrial production [fig. 59-61]. There is no doubt that his theories on the economics of ornament, his realistic principles of artistic economy, had not been abandoned.

fig. 58

ESCOFET TEJERA Y C.ª

Dibujo N.º 1017

MADRID BARCELONA SEVILLA

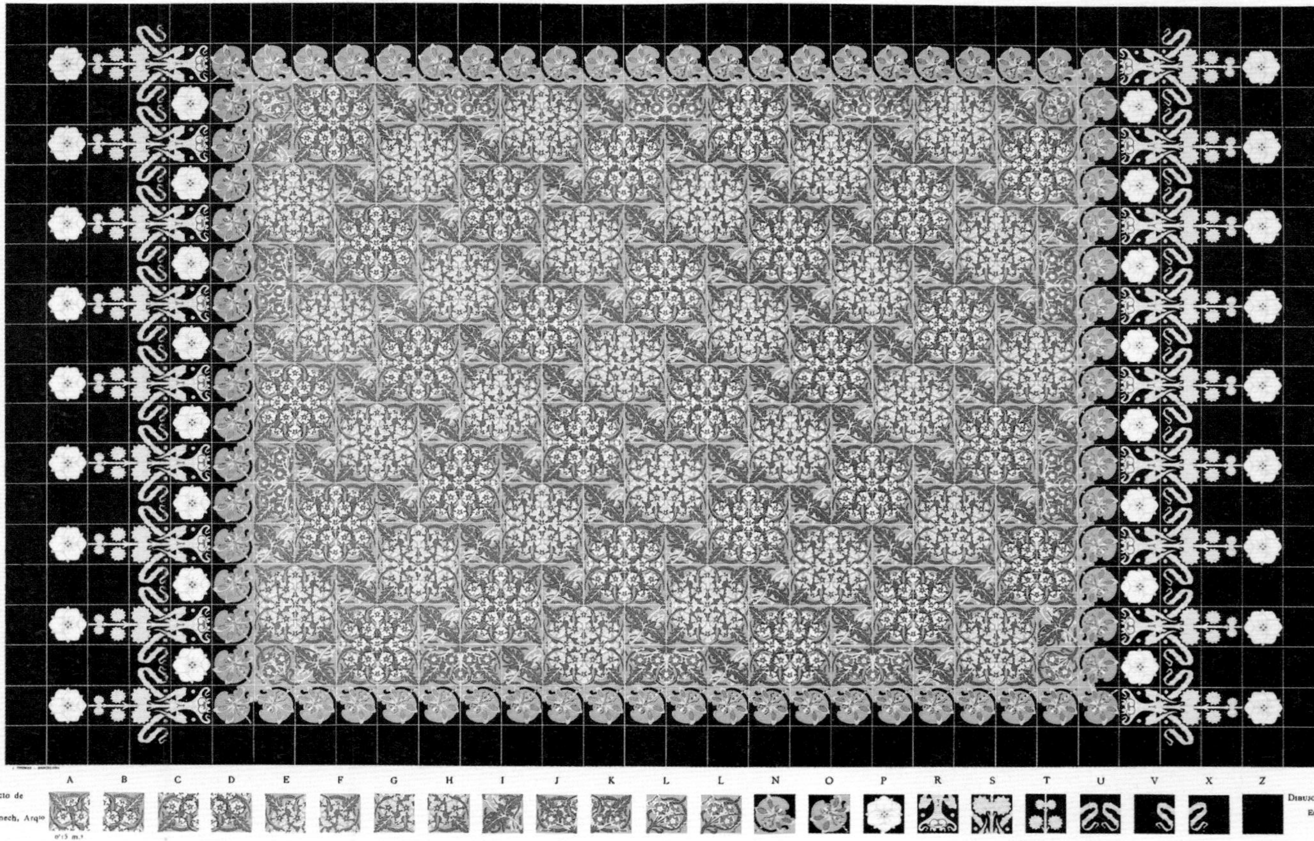

Proyecto de Luis Domenech, Arqto

Dibujo registrado

Escala 1 : 10

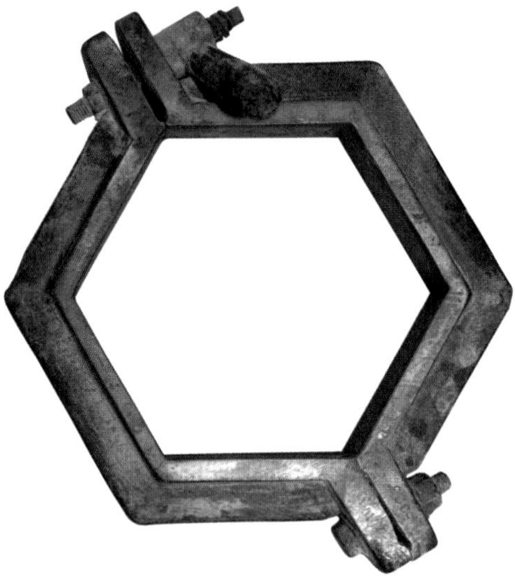

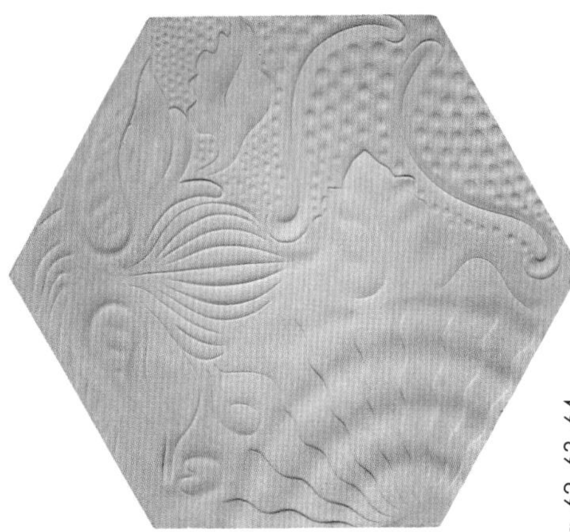

following pages fig. 62, 63, 64

fig. 59, 60, 61

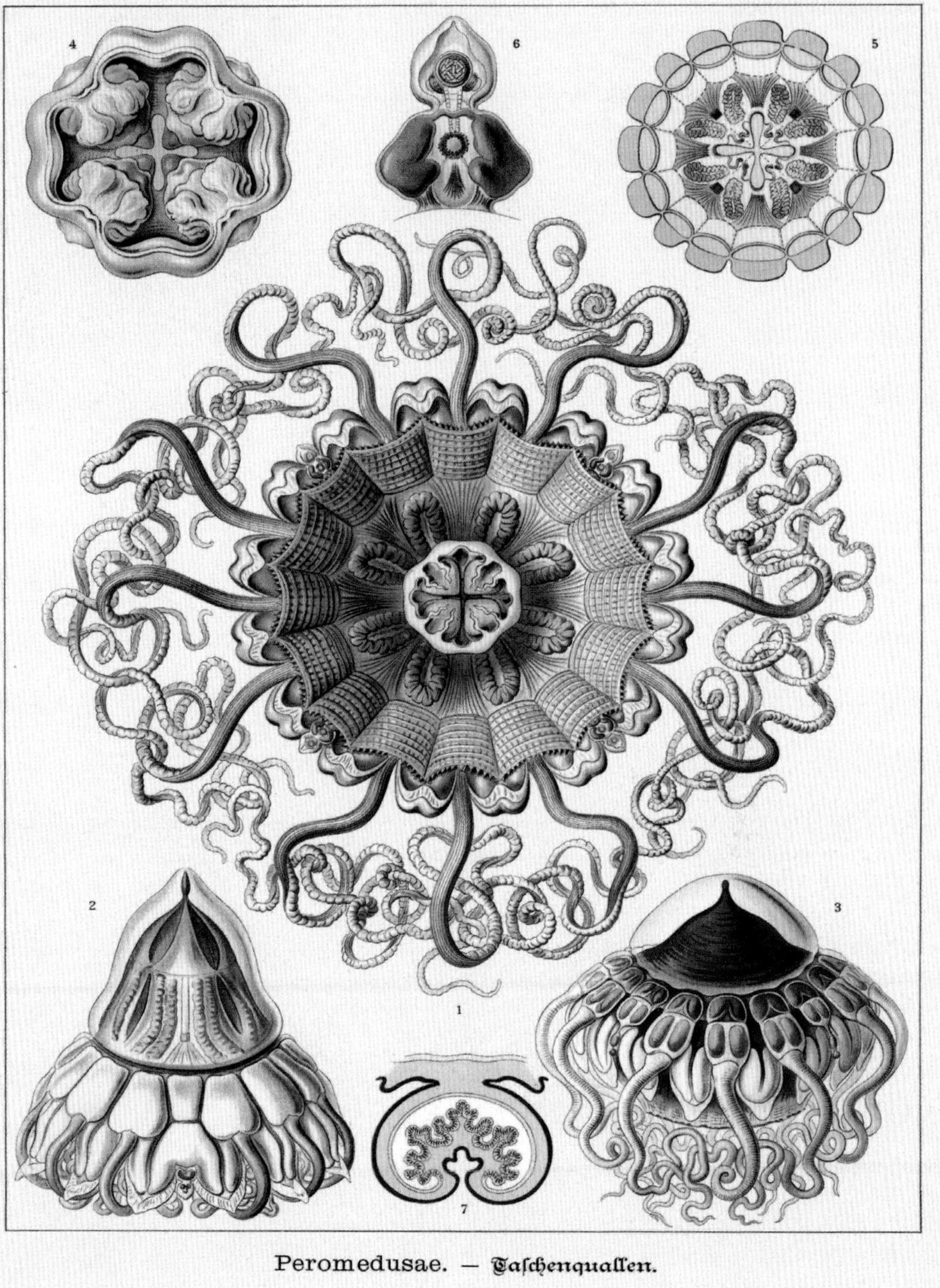

Peromedusae. — Taschenquallen.

Trachomedusae. — Kolbenquallen.

'LA PÂTISSERIE BARCELONE'

'Who is building your house, Domènech, Gaudí or Puig i Cadafalch?' an eager individual in a torn coat asks an elegantly dressed gentleman (the latter perhaps excessively affected, rather too fashionable, slightly foppish: the contrast between the two is essential) in a cartoon by Picarol (Josep Costa Ferrer) published in *L'Esquella de la Torratxa* in October 1905 [fig. 65].[24] The cautious response—'I have yet to decide ... Whoever should win the competition'—refers, like the rest of the jokes on the page, to 'that competition for buildings and façades', the annual prize that Barcelona City Council awarded to the best new building constructed in the city, which had first been won in 1899 by Gaudí's Calvet house [fig. 100], and was then, in 1905, about to be given to the Lleó Morera house by none other than Domènech i Montaner [fig. 78, 79].

In the three cartoons at the foot of the page Picarol depicted the award ceremony. In the first the smiling façades of adjacent buildings beam with expectation; the despondent faces of those that end up without even a consolation prize show their disappointment in the last. In the first scene their crests are festive, like fancy party hats or even crowns, adorned with battlements, buttresses and undulating fleurons, one topped by a cornet that actually breaks through the frame of the cartoon; in the last, however, these cheerful, excessively exuberant forms have been swept away, and the gable of one house, a lank centre-parted thatch, indicates the decline and fall of all things: the tears flowing from the open windows, and the portals like glum mouths, drooping ruefully to the ground.

SOBRE AIXO DEL CONCURS DE EDIFICIS Y FATXADAS

Construccions que aspiran al primer premi.

—¿Sab qué pensava, senyora Tuyas? Que si 'ns presentessim al Concurs de Fatxadas potser ens tocaría alguna cosa.

—Ja ho vaig dir á la "peña" del "Ateneo". Fem la casa nova que potser ens la premiarán y 'ns sortirá mes barata...
—Lo mateix els deya jo á "La Casa del Poble".

—¿Qui us la fa la casa, en Doménech, en Gaudí ó en Puig y Cadafalch?
—Encare no estich ben decidit... El que resulti premiat en el Concurs.

—¿De hont vens, desgraciat, ab aquesta fesomía?
—Veurás: vull concorre al Certámen de fatxadas, y me 'n he fet fer una de nova.

Esperant el premi.

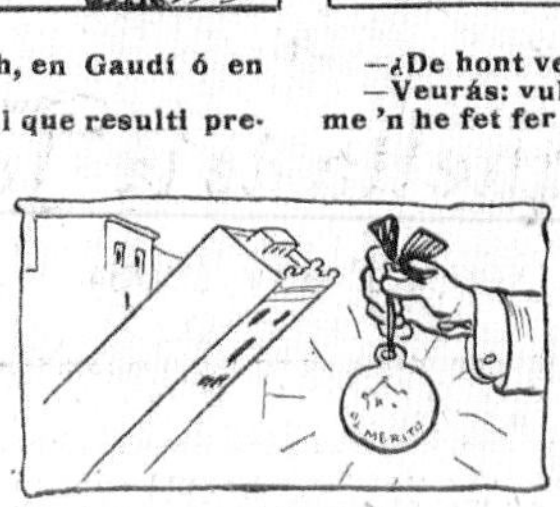

L' acte de la condecoració.

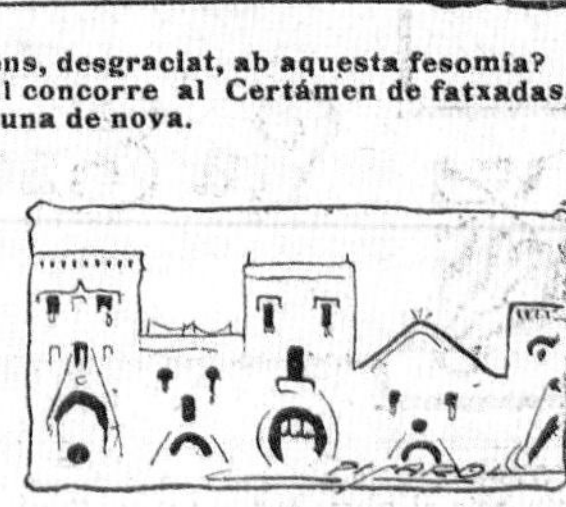

¡Ni un accéssit!

In fact it is not very difficult to recognize in these façades—more precisely, in their linear sequence—something familiar: the triangular gable is not at all common on the streets of Barcelona, a notable exception being the Amatller house [fig. 67, 68], completed by Puig in 1900; one of the mournful mouths, perfectly round, is reminiscent of the highly distinctive balconies on the third floor of the Lleó Morera house, with which Domènech, as I said, won the prize for the best construction completed in 1905, while the others, softened and lengthened by the wrinkles sloping down from the nose, call to mind the keel-shaped openings of the glazed gallery of the Batlló house, which Gaudí was to finish a few months later, in early 1906, popularly known as 'the house of bones' and also, less tragically, as 'the house of yawns'; finally, in such company, what does the conical turret that rises from the corner of one of the façades recall but the tower of the Batlló house [fig. 69-72], which was already at that time, like the glazed gallery, perfectly visible?

So, then, the façades in the Picarol cartoon, in which a number of different but very specific elements seem to have come together as a result of some sort of involuntary automatic reflex—architecture of manic forms, anthropomorphic compositions, fascias deformed by a mood, by laughter or weeping, but in any case deformed (I am not exaggerating here)—evoke, side by side, a very specific place in the Barcelona of that autumn of 1905: the odd-numbered side of the Passeig de Gràcia, Barcelona's most elegant boulevard at the time, between carrer Aragó and carrer Consell de Cent [fig. 66].

On the page of Picarol cartoons everyone is talking about the 'façade prizes', everyone has something to say about them: ladies, gentlemen and maids. And the man in rags refers by name to three of the architects who had built or were building houses on that famous Passeig de Gràcia block—famous, of course, thanks to them, because in effect it was not the prizes that aroused so much interest but, as the down-and-out's question indicated, the architects themselves or, to be more exact, their rivalry.

For example: a contemporary postcard, published by Jorge Venini and entitled 'Paseo de Gracia. Set of modern constructions', shows a perspective of the façades from a point high up on the opposite side of the street [fig. 66]. The explanatory text on the back is highly revealing: 'This block of houses,' it says, 'is notable for offering models of different architectural styles, all original.' It continues, in idiosyncratic syntax: 'During the time of the houses' construction it was commonly called the block of discord for their being different architects and which would be found most pleasing.'

fig. 65

BARCELONA 86 - Paseo de Gracia. Conjunto de construcciones modernas
86 - Promenejo de Gracia. Aro da modernaj konstruaĵoj.

A. T. V.— 2010 - BARCELONA
Construcciones modernas
Paseo de Gracia num. 41
Arquitecto: J. Puig y Cadafalch

fig. 66, 67, 68

fig. 69, 70, 71, 72

This text, I insist, is printed on the back of a postcard, so its purpose is directly linked to the card itself: first, to record the landmarks by which the locals recognize their own city and identify with it; secondly, to travel, to be seen by people far from Barcelona as a message from the city, literally as an advertisement for it. And even more: in this case, the explanatory text, rather verbose in relation to the usual brevity of the medium, deciphers the image more fully than one would expect; it tells us not only what we are seeing, but what it means. How are we to understand this surprising form of *amplificatio* but as a very direct manifestation of the collective unconscious of the city, as a revelation of its *imaginary* at that time, at that precise moment? The architectonic anthropomorphism of Picarol's automata reflects similar issues. The houses that we see there, the postcard tells us, were taking part in a competition of their own, a fiercely contested competition with no other rules than rivalry itself, or *discord*, in which the jury was the opinion of the public circulating on the street in front of them. It was for the universal and anonymous public that they had been built, these houses, all *different* and all *original*: to be the *most* pleasing.

But what are we describing? Commercial competition, the law of supply and demand, a mass public ... Since the end of the *ancien régime* and all through the nineteenth century artists had seen how the forms of patronage through which they had traditionally connected with the world had been replaced, as had happened in other sectors of society, by market forces. Artists no longer depended on their personal relationship with a patron, a prince or an institution for whom they acted as servant, jester, courtier or functionary, nor could they claim prestige on the strength of their knowledge of a shared collective discipline that coincided with the ideological and symbolic programmes—also collective—of their clients; in fact, they could not even hope for such things. Like every other trade and profession, theirs had been stripped of *protection*, had been commodified, and their product, the artwork, converted irreversibly into merchandise; it had become anonymous, like the bourgeoisie that could afford to consume it and to whom it was touted by a new breed of intermediaries: galleries, dealers, magazines ... In this new environment, the artists and their commentators adopted—as they had no choice but to do—perfectly circular strategies that were as *modern* as the mechanisms of the market themselves: exorcistic imprecations against the turning of art into a commodity that sought, rhetorically, to make the *necessary* modernity of the market art's greatest virtue. Bohemianism, the theory of *l'art pour l'art*, scandal, a sneering contempt for the bourgeoisie: all of these traits of identity so characteristic of the aristocratizing haute bourgeoisie of the second half of the nineteenth century serve equally to define the modern artist and his (rarely her) public. By what other means and with what other principles could such a hugely important and at the same time marginal market sector, that of luxury goods, be monopolized or very nearly monopolized? It is here that consumption attains its highest tones, in being made *transcendent* by the work of the artist. Propaganda technique: the modern artist is an eccentric who does not work for the public but imposes his tastes on it. By the early 1900s, when those *different* and *original* houses were being built, the artist was—and had been for some time—a perfectly coded type.

The great complexity of a work of architecture, its high cost in money, labour and time, and its reliance on craftsmanship and technique kept the architect linked for longer to the institution and the academy and thus to some extent protected from the harshest realities of competition. By the turn of the century, however, the growth of the construction market in the major European capitals and the emerging need for self-representation of urban societies based unambiguously on mass consumption, propaganda and spectacle were putting an end to that privileged situation. Somewhat belatedly, then, when all of the mannerisms of the *modern* artist had become stereotypes, the architects in their turn had to become adherents of the religion of art for art's sake. And they did so, of course, with all the conviction of the neophyte: the modern architect is one who not only assumes responsibility for the planning and construction of the building, as had more or less always been the case, but is also able to go much further, expending maximum creative energy on elements hitherto considered minor or secondary and traditionally left to the craftsman or the factory but now, suddenly, placed in the foreground and hailed as essential: railings, grilles, lamps, doorknobs and fingerplates, signs, weathervanes ... This was a delirium *of the author* that architecture had never known before, of course, just as the architect had never before invaded so many areas of life, now taking charge of the furniture, vases, tapestries and carpets, crockery and cutlery, and even sometimes the wardrobe of the lady of the house.

In the cities of Europe in the two decades on either side of 1900 there was a bourgeoisie, in some cases high and in others not so high, ready and willing to shell out for a house conceived in a flash of inspiration, from foundations to lightning rod, and intended to evoke the magnificent mansions of the dandies of *décadentisme*, those obsessive, more than distinctive interiors literally pervaded by the *nervous life* of their inhabitants, in which everything has been personally selected from the world of the richest and most sophisticated objects, and in which the tension of the whole universe, conflated with the mood of the owner, seems always to be

fig. 73, 74, 75

condensed in a single detail: in the frame of a Rococo mirror, in a Japanese fan, in a cameo, in a miniature ... Some of these houses, such as Des Esseintes's, described by Huysmans in *À rebours* (Against Nature), came from the realm of the imagination, while others, like Edmond and Jules de Goncourt's [fig. 73] *hôtel* in Auteuil, were absolutely real—Edmond dedicated a book to it, a sort of catalogue of his treasures full of *impressions* and entitled, not coincidentally, *La Maison d'un Artiste*[25]—but they all shared the same purpose: to present themselves as fortresses closed to the law of universal equivalence imposed by merchandise in the world outside.

These were treasures not just because they were rare and strange but also and especially because they had been chosen out of all the treasures in the world by an owner who had either been possessed by the life of his objects or had given them life by breathing his spirit into them [fig. 74, 75].

Evidently, the town houses of 1900 to which I am referring are simply a more or less exquisite parody of these models and should be seen, indeed, as signifying precisely their inversion, in which the clients have effectively delegated to the artist-architect the expression of their character so that ultimately—as a famous story by Adolf Loos about a 'poor little rich man', which we shall discuss below, explains very well—it is the architects that impose their tastes.[26]

The *fin de siècle* architect followed the model fashioned by the modern artist. He too was an eccentric, competing with others like him in the luxury market, but his field of action made him a far more *dangerous* figure, on that some of the most secret and most terrible conditions of merchandise were manifested through him. What, indeed, could someone who transforms into art everything he touches —a house, a chair, a carpet, a salt cellar, all of life ... —be, but the closest thing to that metaphor of equivalence and of death that we see in King Midas?

The modern architect and modern architecture became social figures, and people on the streets voiced their opinion of the façades as if they were paintings in a Salon exhibition. In establishing a prize for the best building of the year, Barcelona City Council was closely following the example of Brussels and of Paris, which had first awarded such a prize in 1898 to a magnificent and eccentric work: Hector Guimard's Castel Béranger. It is not hard to see that what is being celebrated in these competitions has very little to do with the *publicae venustati* of the ancients and their idea of *decorum*. Instead of extolling the building's adaptation to and compatibility with its place and its function, and rather than exalting collective values, those prizes rewarding, as we have seen, the *different* and the *original*; in other words, the individualism of and the rivalry between owners and architects. That rivalry was to reach ecstatic frenzy in those great showcases of *fin de siècle* architecture, the Paris Exposition of 1889 and, above all, the delirium of the 1900 Exposition [fig. 76, 77].

The millions of visitors who strolled around the extravagant buildings of the latter clearly reflect the two extremes between which the Art Nouveau architect moved: first, the bourgeois salon, where everything must be unique and private, and secondly, the crowds that turn the same architecture, the same supposedly elitist designs, into a great popular spectacle. But these extremes are—perfectly unparadoxically—completely complementary: they are exactly the same as those between which the cycles of fashion oscillate and *operate*, and it was in precisely this period that fashion began to be an essential subject of study for sociologists like Veblen or Simmel and, a little later, Sombart.[27]

Situated at this point, and having rather late in the day taken on the role of the modern artist, which had already become a caricature, the fame of the *fin de siècle* architect and the fortune enjoyed by his works could hardly be more ambiguous: almost always execrated by the serious press, constantly pilloried in the satirical papers, architects were the mandarins of whom Flaubert remarked, in *Le Dictionnaire des idées reçues* (The Dictionary of Received Ideas), 'Architects: All idiots. Always forget to put stairs in their houses.'[28] That, without doubt, is the modern, *popular* form of success.

But let's go back to Barcelona. It was at the end of the nineteenth century, and not before, that an entire generation of the city's bourgeoisie chose to abandon the great houses of the old town in which they had resided until then and move to apartments in the new buildings of the Eixample. *New* buildings, indeed, which they themselves constructed and which, unlike the grand old inherited mansions in the old districts, they were the first to live in; buildings, in short, adapted to their new needs, both functional and, above all, aesthetic. In 1895, in an article dedicated to the modern artist Santiago Rusiñol[29] and tellingly entitled 'Those Who Are Something', Salvador Canals wrote: 'The bourgeois is no longer a manufacturer nor even a banker; He is a man who has style.'[30] In the two decades on either side of 1900 several hundred of these new buildings were constructed in the Eixample. It will come as no surprise that the fashionable outfitters had installed themselves there from the outset, along with the society photographer Audouard,

LA PORTE MONUMENTALE

fig. 76

LE PALAIS DES ILLUSIONS

C'est une vaste salle hexagonale revêtue, sur ses six côtés, d'immenses glaces de Saint-Gobain, et couverte par un plafond doré, sculpté dans le style mauresque par M. Alméras. Une série de lampes électriques, installées avec le plus grand art par MM. Picon et Martine, éclairent de tons variés et changeants des colonnes, des appliques, des girandoles qui se reflètent à l'infini, et donnent l'illusion d'une féerique mosquée illuminée de cent mille feux.

fig. 77

Al Padre Santo de Roma

I

No le dieron el cetro la intriga,
ni la torpe ambición, ni el engaño,
ni la sangre que vierten los hombres
que se roban el oro y el mando.
Dios lo puso de todos los tronos
en el trono más puro y más alto,
y subió como siervo que sube
con la cruz del deber al Calvario.
¡Y subió con el santo derecho
del Príncipe santo,
sin la náusea de odio en el alma,
sin la mueca del triunfo en los labios,
sin mancha en la frente,
sin sangre en las manos!...
Era el trono entre Dios y los hombres
dulcísimo lazo,
Para-rayos divino del mundo,
concordia entre hermanos,
faro en las tinieblas,
orden en el caos.

—

Y el Ungido miraba á sus hijos,
y lloraba de amor al mirarlos...
¡Tan débiles todos!...
¡Todos tan amados!...
Y tornaba los ojos al cielo,
y alzaba los brazos,
y del cielo á raudales caían,
al subir la oración de sus labios,
luces en su mente,
bienes en sus manos...
Y en la grada más alta del trono
mirando hacia abajo,
temblando de amores,
de amores llorando...
Soberano, radiante, divino,
sublime, inspirado,
como blanca visión de los cielos,
como Padre de amores avaro,
que á sus hijos quisiera traerles
la gloria en pedazos...
dulce, generoso,
solemne, magnánimo,
derramaba la luz de su mente
y el bien de sus manos,
inundando de efluvios de cielo
del mundo los ámbitos.

II

¡Se resiste la mente á creerlo!
¡Se resiste la lira á cantarlo!
La legión de los hombres impíos,
la legión de los hijos ingratos,
ante el trono del Príncipe justo,
del Príncipe sabio,
ante el trono del Padre amoroso,
del Padre injuriado,
congregados por vientos de abismo,
rugieron, gritaron...
¡Lo mismo que aquellos
que escuchaba el cobarde Pilatos!
Y rodó la corona del justo,
y á la cárcel al justo llevaron,
¡y vive en la cárcel por ellos gimiendo,
por todos orando!

—

¡Se resiste á creerlo la mente!
¡Se resiste la lira á cantarlo!
Y una sola cuerda,
que responde al pulsarla mi mano,
sólo quiere cantar esta estrofa,
que repite con ecos airados:
«¡Ay de los impíos!
¡ay de los ingratos
que coronan de agudas espinas
las sienes de un santo,
la frente de un Padre,
la cabeza de un débil anciano!»

GABRIEL Y GALÁN

LA CONSTRUCCIÓN MODERNA EN BARCELONA

Concurso de edificios y establecimientos urbanos

Primer premio: Casa n.° 35 del Paseo de Gracia, proyectada y dirigida por el arquitecto señor Domenech y Muntaner

(Fotografía P. Reig)

Los nidos del Capitolio

Cuando los Galos, antiguos moradores de la vecina Francia, asaltaron y destruyeron á Roma, los habitantes de esta ciudad que pudieron salvarse de la muerte se refugiaron en el Capitolio, que era á la vez templo grandioso y fortaleza inexpugnable. En los huecos, aleros y cornisas de este edificio, levantado en honor de Júpiter, formaban sus nidos muchas y hermosas aves consagradas al dios de aquel nombre; y aunque los romanos todos miraban con gran veneración los ocultos albergues de estos pájaros, á veces los soldados que estaban de guardia en las almenas de la fortificación se permitían ejercitar

fig. 79, 80, previous page fig. 78

BARCELONA FUTURA

El veritable destí
del casal d'en Milà y Pi.

GITANADA

Es tant lo que procuro per la Capital meva
que he fet moltes consultes per sebre el seu Destí,
y al fi he trobat un *paio* dels quins fumen la breva
que, pagantla nosaltres, sols ens toca escupí.

Sabent el que cercava, m'ha dit tot campetxano:
—Si hi ha bona propina jo el posaré al corrent.—
Y al veure que a l'armilla duia la mà, el *gitano,*
parant les seves dugues, ha prosseguit dient:

—La pobre Barcelona fa temps que està sumissa
pels desenganys que porta y el mal que d'ella han dit;
tothom diu que l'estima y cap la fa felissa;
de pretendents n'hi sobren, mes cap es bon partit.

La volteja un fulano que va vestit de negre
que diu que es moralista y sempre hi va ab sermons,
perquè deixi depressa la seva vida alegre
y sols rumbegi en temples de Deu y en processons.

Si pogués ell ser l'amo jo crec que a aquestes hores
la Meller y Escribano tindria en un convent,
perquè segons confessa les troba *superiores*
y creu que allí estarien dintre del seu ambient.

També la volta un *paio* que be prou l'amanyaga
per més que es un subjecte dels més esbojarrats,
puig que molts cops, la pobre, després que'l gasto paga,
l'amenassa ab cremarla per tots quatre costats.

Hi ha un soci que hi rodeja carregat de mils duros
que ensenyar molt les barres tot sovint se li acut;
aquet diu que l'estima, que la treurà d'apuros
prò'm sembla que li renta la cara ab un drap brut.

Y, finalment, hi ha un jove, que's veu que ella s'hi arrima,
perquè es tot honradesa y es forsut esquerrà,
que res li dol per ella perquè de cor l'estima,
prò els altres tres li priven de que obtingui sa mà.

D'aquestos que s'hi oposen tant ella n'està cuita
que, com nou Samsó, un dia farà un suprem esfors,
y enderrocant el temple farà d'ells una truita
perquè el pas no obstrueixin dels seus bons aimadors.

¡Ai fill meu! t'asseguro que ella, de dia en dia,
recobra noves forses pel baf de llibertat
y un cop recuperada ja tota sa energia
veuras com per les rates sabrà trobà un bon gat.

No dubtis pas d'aquesta verídica planeta,
puig sé que tu l'estimes y això't deixa content;
allarga la propina, no't dolgui una pesseta,
que es el primer cop, *paio,* que'l meu llavi no ment.—

. . . .

Vaig darli lo que duia, content d'aquet fulano,
per veurhi en ses paraules molta sinceritat.
¡Que fora bell—pensava—si acas aquet *gitano*
parlant de Barcelona no hagués *gitanejat!*

MARTÍ REVOLTÓS

for example, on the ground floor of the Lleó Morera house [fig. 79], and the film and phonograph company Pathé Frères in the Batlló house [fig. 80]. The great need for collective legitimization felt by this generation of the bourgeoisie and its members' particular desire for distinction thus coincided with an unprecedented quantity of new building.

Quantity, on one hand, and quality as the paroxysm of a *new style* on the other: no wonder, then, that in the Barcelona of those years there should appear that personage with upper-class bohemian airs—and at the same time, the vaudeville caricature—that is the modern architect, known locally as *Modernista*. Nor is it surprising that in those years, a few works of architecture should have become subjects of popular opinion. Here again we need only leaf through the satirical press to encounter them: the streetlights on the Passeig de Gràcia [fig. 82, 83] and the monument by Pere Falqués to the playwright Pitarra [fig. 84-87], or the Sagrada Família by Gaudí [fig. 97] and, a little later, his Milà house [fig. 81, 103-105, 110] are among the outstanding examples. But none of these has what made Barcelona's 'block of *discord*'* the perfect paradigm of the situation we are considering here: the manifest presence of discord, precisely: the absolutely explicit rivalry here between architects or, even better, between their façades. What is more, not only do these three houses stand side by side, like pictures at an exhibition, but they also do so, in a defining manner, in the right place at the right time: the Passeig de Gràcia was, in 1900, the showcase chosen by that bourgeois generation of which we have spoken to display its new—modern—habits of representation and consumption; in other words, its style.

The façades shown in the Picarol cartoons were, it is worth recalling, faces capable of showing their feelings. In 1906, in a cartoon in *El Diluvio* with the caption 'New Barcelona', Brunet—who a few years later was to draw some of the cruellest caricatures of the Milà house— depicted 'projects for *Modernista* buildings / that various artists will construct here' [fig. 88].[31]

---

* TN: Spanish *manzana* translates both as 'block', in the sense of a compact mass of buildings, and as 'apple', so that *manzana de la discordia* is also 'apple of discord', a reference to the apple thrown down by Eris at the wedding of Peleus and Thetis, provoking a quarrel between Athena, Hera and Aphrodite, the Judgement of Paris and, as a consequence of this, the Trojan War.

fig. 81

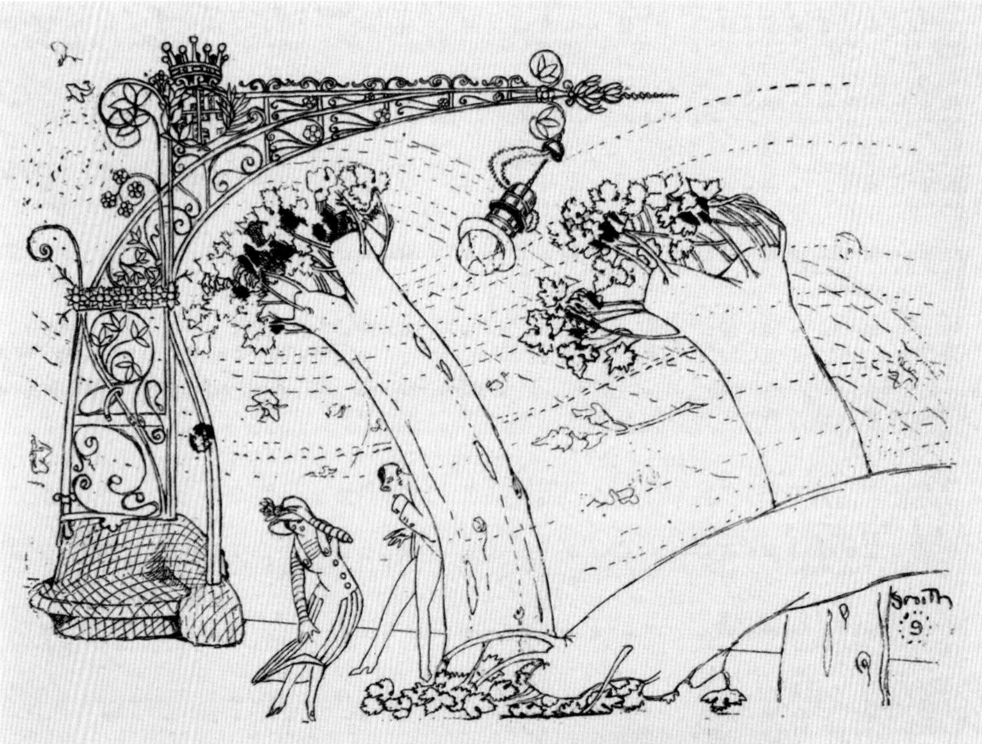

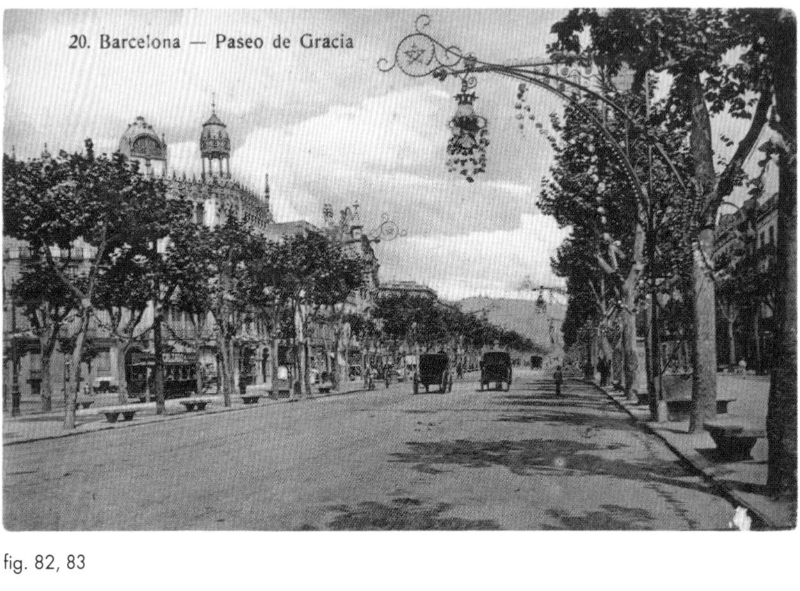
20. Barcelona — Paseo de Gracia

fig. 82, 83

fig. 84, 85, 86, 87, following pages fig. 88

Dos devotas salen de San Jaime encomiando las excelencias de un sermon predicado por cierto franciscano.

—¡Hija, qué bien habla ese hombre!

—En mi vida he oído cosas mejores sobre la caridad.

- Tienes razon; despues de oir esto dan ganas de repartir á los pobres hasta la camisa que una lleva.

Un chiquillo lleno de harapos se pone delante de ellas y dice:

—¡Señoritas, una limosna por amor de Dios!

Las dos á un tiempo:

—¡Aparta, granuja!

FRAY GERUNDIO.

El «Raja» y el «Colorao»

— Adios, *Raja!*
- *¡Colorao!*
¡Gracias á Dios que te encuentro!
—¿Pus qué te pasa?
—¡El delirio!
—¿Has regañao con la *Pelos?*
—A medias.
—Pus habla, hombre;
ya sabes que yo te aprecio
y tó lo que á tí te ocurre
me afezta.
—Pus mi deseo
era encontrarte así, á solas,
pá que tú, que tiés cerebro,
despues de escuchar mis penas,
me dieras algun consejo.
—Habla ya. Pero ¿estás lívido?
—¡Si es que tengo encima el vértigo
dende que esa mala... perra
me ha hecho lo que me ha hecho.
—¿Tan grave es?
—Vamos, hombre;
con el genio que yo tengo...
yo no sé cómo á estas horas
no he salido en *Los Sucesos.*
Figúrate que ayer tarde
iba fuerte de chaleco,
y como por esa golfa
estoy bebiendo los vientos,
dije entre mí: Nada *Raja*,
hoy vas á hacerle un obsequio
á tu gachí...
—¿Y le compraste?...
—Un pito de á real y medio
—¡Gachó! ¡Te arruinarías!
¡Vaya un regalo soberbio!
—Pero si es que por los pitos
se desvive la muy... *Pelos.*
Pus bien; iba yo pá casa
con el pito, tan contento.
Subo la escalera aprisa,
deseando ver el efezto.
Voy á llamar y oigo dentro
la voz de un hombre. ¡Calcula
tú mi sorpresa y mi!...
—¡Cuerno!
—Eso fué lo que yo dije.
Iba á echar la puerta al suelo,
pero me contuve. Aquí,
pensé, hay que tener criterio.
—¿Y el pito?
- Pus en la mano.
—*Prosigüe.*
A todo esto
apliqué el oído al ojo
de la cerradura, atento
escuchando, á ver en qué
acabaría tó aquello,
y oí como el muy... lechon
le decía así á la *Pelos:*

BAR

EDIFICIO PÚBLICO MUNIC

Proye
que

LONA NUEVA

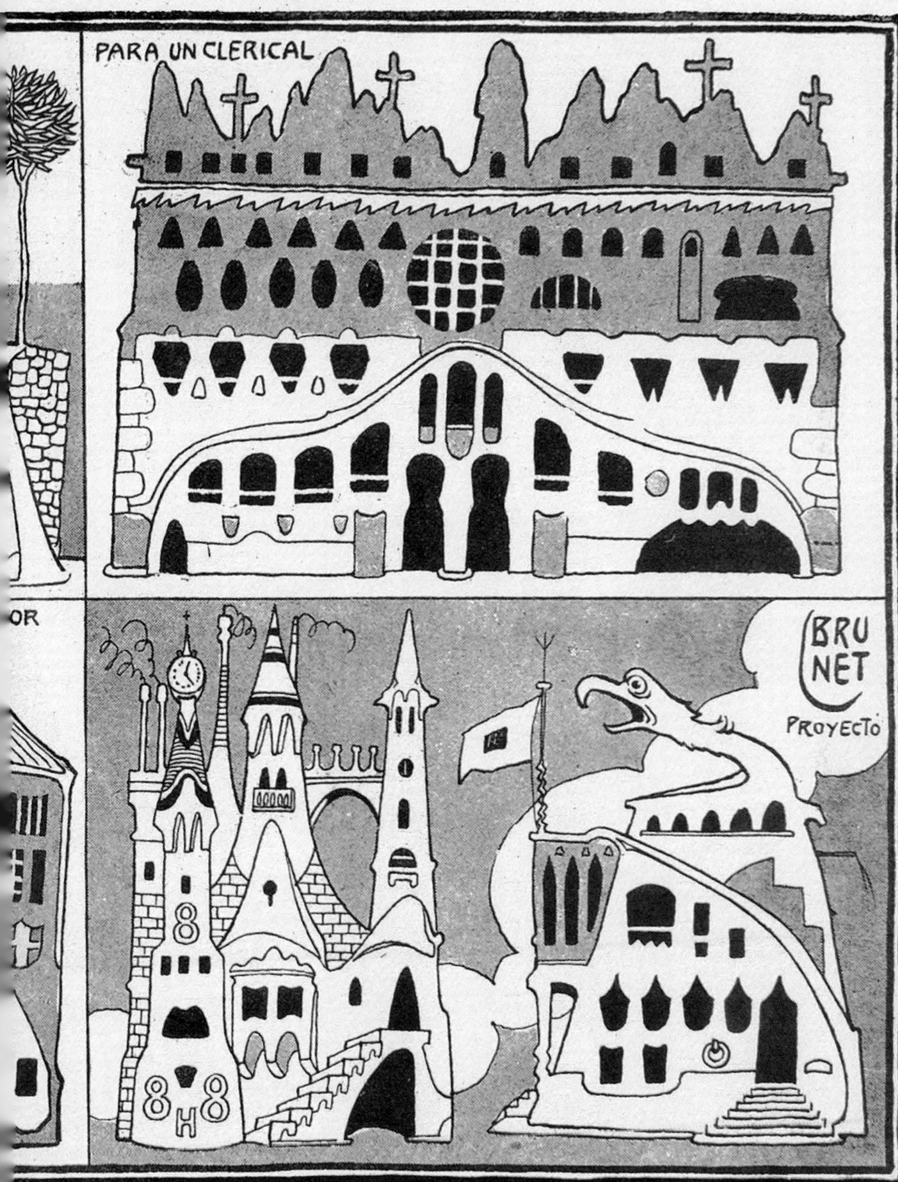

PARA UN FABRICANTE

PARA UN POLITICO

dificios modernistas
n aquí varios artistas.

fig. 89, 90

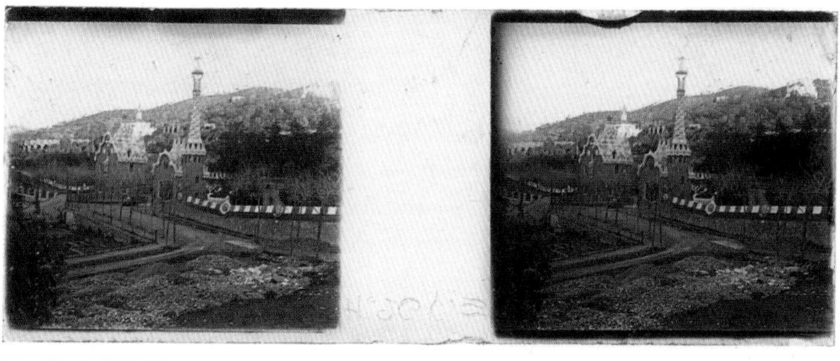

fig. 91, 92, 93

These new projects are actually façades, and most of them also have facial features. In addition to the strange openings, the spiky tops of towers and spires (or newels), the rooftops of cream or snow and the general softening of the forms, they have animals living on them and plants growing on them. It is not difficult to perceive in these hybrids of enchanted castle, gingerbread house, zoo and greengrocer's shop an essentially Gaudí-esque air, a comical blend of the Park Güell gatehouses [fig. 89-93] and the Batlló house, in the main. Even more explicitly, one of the façades is crowned with the profile of the mountain of Montserrat topped by several crosses; that these are not four-armed makes the reference no less obvious. But the point is that these projects—all but one, which is ostensibly for a 'municipal public building'—have been designed for a few typical characters: an industrialist, a farmer, a cleric, a manufacturer, a politician. Brunet is mocking here not only the *Modernista* style but also the pretentiousness of making one's house the expression of one's character, made possible, of course, by the madness of architects who are modern because they are eccentric and eccentric because they are modern.

The fact that all forms, all signs and all symbols, even the most seemingly obvious and traditional (including the most sacred), have become trademarks—of Gaudí in particular—is precisely the gist of another cartoon, by Apa (Feliu Elias), published in *Papitu* in January 1909, in which the architect, explaining the plan of his project to the parish priest, says, 'You see here at the top a cross so that Our Lord will protect the house from lightning,' and the priest replies, 'Yes, yes, very good; and on top of the cross a lightning rod, don't you think?'[32] [fig. 89, 94, 95] What the modern architect imposes on the client is his delirious subjectivity, in a juggling act in which forms, symbols and meanings are all up in the air, in defiance of the traditional decorum that made the correspondence between those things precisely the virtue of a building. At the same time, though, that is what the client is buying: a very, very expensive subjectivity.

The gentleman in the Picarol cartoon, in view of the choices available, had yet to make up his mind. But that is the market and its mechanisms: Domènech, Gaudí, Puig ...? Whoever wins the competition! Of course: but in that competition Antoni 0 Gaudí had the advantage.

He started designing his building four years after Puig's was completed and a year after Domènech started his. He was therefore the only one who knew what the others had done: and what they had done, especially Puig in 1900, with the inaugural triangular crown of the Amatller house, was distinguish themselves from the mass

164 PAPITU

"Un diputado solidario"

Recentment, el diputat solidari per Vilademuls, en Bofarull, ha dirigit als seus electors un manifest. El manifest estava redactat en parla cervantesca. El senyor Bofarull, encare creu que fa més fi'l castellá, fins dirigintse als pagesos; el senyor Bofarull ignora qu'es un'alta cursilería fer l'elegant en llengua que per Vilademuls no parlen més que'ls recaudadors de contribució y els carrabiners de Cadaqués y Rosas.

La Veu se queixava l'altre día de que'ls forners usaven en els seus actes el castellá, una llengua impropia d'ells, y *La Veu* que ha sabut veure l'antagonisme entre'l castellá y els llonguets, no té ni una ínfima censura pera un diputat solidari que pera que no's perdi la tradició dels «cuneros» escriu en castellá les seves escritures polítiques' Peró'l senyor Bofarull que té ben poques coses que explicar al seu districte tal volta fa això pera que no l'entenguin.

L'Arquitecte.—Veu y a dalt de tot una creu perque Deu N. S. preservi al edifici del llamp
El Rector.—Si, si, molt bé; y a demunt de la creu un parallamps ¿no li sembla?

fig. 94, 95

of conventional buildings in the neoclassical tradition with which the Eixample had been constructed over the previous forty years. In effect, that stepped gable abruptly interrupted not only the horizontal continuity of the balustrades of the neighbouring houses but also—and quite deliberately—that of the whole Eixample. Domènech, with the unusual form and composition of the voids of the Lleó Morera house and its decorative spectacularity, would subsequently pursue the same goal [fig. 78, 79]. For both, then, it was a question of placing themselves above what most of the Barcelona *intelligyentsia* of the time regarded as routine conformity, as the lack of imagination of the buildings that filled the Eixample, which also, reduced to the isotropy of its grid, was already inevitably in their eyes a place of monotony with no prospects.

Even in 1912, Francesc Pujols[33] could write in *Picarol*, in his commentary on the ardent works of architecture drawn by Josep Aragay [fig. 96]: 'The architects of the city of Barcelona are: 1st, Mr Gaudí; 2nd, Mr Domènech i Montaner, and 3rd, Mr Puig i Cadafalch. Which is the boldest? We do not know. All three are setting the city on fire ...'[34] We shall leave for the next chapter our discussion of the complex implications of the continuation of the Pujols text, in which he compares our three personages to the revolutionaries who had set fire to churches and presents them as the 'true architects of Barcelona's constant revolution'. What concerns us now is the image of buildings in flames, an unconscious metaphor for the city that endlessly consumes itself, always turning into its own spectacle, and thus a metaphor of the modern market-city, lively and cosmopolitan, of which those intellectuals—in many cases far removed not only from the real material possibilities but also from the true desires of its bourgeoisie—dreamed, to the construction, or at least the suggestion of which, those architects were called.

It is in this generic perspective that we must frame the splendour of the houses by Domènech and Puig: there is no denying the rivalry between their works, or that both strove to exhibit an individual *originality* and a specific richness that derives from both the architect and the client, but this rivalry was in some sense indirect, because their ultimate purpose— their higher purpose, we might say—was to confront, in order to correct, the provincialism and the lack of monumentality that they saw as having made the Eixample, for so many years, a place without qualities, anonymous.

Can the same be said of Gaudí, the last to arrive on the 'block of discord'? To begin with, we must not forget that he was not constructing a new building but reforming an existing one, one of these houses with regular balconies supported by cornices and topped by balustrades. Accordingly, his confrontation with the neoclassical rhythm of the Eixample façades was not a purely creative exercise but a problem of contact, and Gaudí interpreted it as such: as a real effort, physical work aimed at materially eradicating the earlier construction. This could not be transformed by a simple superposition, the application of a new skin or a mask, because Gaudí thought of it not as a composition but as a material mass that could only be combatted vehemently. Without demolishing it—that is the important point—Gaudí strove to leave not a trace of the old house. Perhaps the vision of bricklayers standing on the scaffolding and hammering away at the brick wall, knocking it back to achieve the undulating surface Gaudí wanted, constitutes the most vivid image of how he must have seen that confrontation: not as a generic intellectual issue but as a hand-to-hand combat fought there and then, in that place and at that time [fig. 98, 99].

Gaudí understood the relationship of his work with the neighbouring houses, and especially, of course, with Puig i Cadafalch's Amatller house, in exactly the same way, as a matter of contact. As has so often been pointed out, on the top floor of the building Gaudí removed the balcony abutting on the Amatller house to create a little terrace, set back somewhat from the façade, and from the side of this terrace opposite the party wall there rises the cylindrical tower that culminates in the cross. So the two houses meet flush at this point at which the sharp moulding of the right-angled crown of the Amatller house is folded over by the Batlló house, a soft band of stone whose ends close in tight spirals. Finally, on the Batlló crown Gaudí repeats the triangular form—very rare in Barcelona, as I have said—of the Amatller house, but now the wall has become a mansard and the rectangular flat steps transformed into the undulating volume of a roof [fig. 94].

The contrast between the symmetrical gable of the Amatller house and the ambiguous asymmetry and rippling motion of the Batlló house causes an abrupt jolting sensation. We could say that with this lateral shift, in which the pre-existing form of the Amatller house can still be divined, the Batlló house literally edges up on its neighbour: Gaudí's moulding does not so much meet Puig i Cadafalch's as touch it, like a furtively outstretched hand. But at the same time the roof of the Batlló house, its hat, rises above the crown of its neighbour, while, higher still, directly over the little terrace at which the two houses abut, rises the tower crowned with a four-armed cross, already famous, even then, as a Gaudí trademark.

following pages fig. 96, 97

Dibuix d'en Josep Aragay

Els arquitectes de la ciutat de Barcelona són: 1.er, el senyor Gaudí; 2.on, el senyor Domènec i Montaner, i 3.er, el senyor Puig i Cadafalc. Quin es el més atrevit? No ho sabem. Tots tres encenen la ciutat en flames. Així com els que van fer la segona crema de convents encenían la ciutat en flames destruint, aquests tres arquitectes l'encenen construint. Tant els uns com els altres són uns revolucionaris com una casa, sinó que'ls uns fan la revolució des de baix, o des del carrer, i els altres des de dalt dels edificis que aixequen.

Veritables arquitectes de la revolució continua barcelonina, perpetúen en pedres i maons l'ànima que'ns aguanta, i tenen el valor de tornar a començar com si res hagués succeït. El senyor Puig i Cadafalc torna a començar per l'Edat Mitjana; el senyor Domènec i Montaner s'allarga fins a certes i determinades èpoques, i el senyor Gaudí, defugint compromisos, s'arriba fins a la prehistoria, i pera un home tant conegut com el senyor Milà, improvisa un edifici, les arrels del qual se perden en la nit dels temps. D'això se'n diu tornar a començar. No extranyin, doncs, l'aspecte que presenta aquest magnífic dibuix que publiquem. Es un aspecte de Barcelona flamejanta.

PALAU DE LA ARQUITECTURA CATALANA
DEL G. A. M. SR. GAUDÍ

Although on the other side of the façade of the Batlló house a cylindrical moulding also seems to stop at—or trip over—the cornice and mouldings of the thoroughly conventional neighbouring building, forming soft accretions of stone, it is clear that what really interested Gaudí here were the singularities—the originality—of the Amatller house. It is to this, as we have seen, that the complex forms of its crown allude, and with this that its movements seek closer contact. At the same time, and above all, it is from this that they most manifestly depart: they refer to it and retain, very faintly, like remote traces or, better yet, like vague reflections in a clouded or distorting mirror, some of its most striking forms, thus making even clearer the contrast and the separation of the two that will eventually take place. In other words, the originality of the Batlló house is defined, at least initially, but certainly, at the expense of the adjacent Amatller house, as emulation — but as exaggerated emulation, literally as *its* extravagance. Buried at the bottom of the softened forms of the Batlló house there lie not only the neoclassical building that Gaudí was commissioned to remodel [fig. 67, 98, 99] but also the Amatller house, which still stands alongside it.

In Gaudí's case the order of direct and indirect rivalry we commented on in relation to the works of Domènech and Puig is reversed. The pressing physical contact with things that he imposed made what was closest essential. Gaudí's rivals, with whom he was consciously competing in the 'block of discord', could only be his peers: modern architects. The manner in which he, the last to arrive, as I said, treats the Amatller house, the way he devours and digests it, the way he sinks it beneath the disproportionate, excessive—and soft!—forms of his house could not be more eloquent. The caption on that postcard tells us that while the houses were being built, people wondered 'which would be found most pleasing'. The market—competition—was a latter-day Eris that no longer needed an invitation to leave, here or there, again and again, the golden apple *for the most beautiful,* and the latter-day Paris was the passer-by on the street. The 'block of discord' is where at the start of the twentieth century the rivalry between Barcelona's modern architects manifested itself, the place where the new rules of a renewed profession were first placed on the table, or before the eyes of the public, not because first Puig and then Domènech constructed two fine houses there, five years and fifty metres removed from one another, but precisely because Gaudí, facing them off with his Batlló house, played the card of discord. The 'block of discord' exists because Gaudí built the Batlló house.

Gaudí perfectly represents the role of the modern, *Modernista* architect. On one hand, *upstairs,* imposing his taste, laden with excesses, on the things that pertain directly to daily life—to the private life of his clients, of course, but also to the public life of their city—he carried to the limit the *modus operandi* of the *fin-de-siècle* bohemian artist, the grand bourgeois; on the other hand, *downstairs*, the judgement passed on his work by the anonymous public, members of a society based now on consumption and spectacle, made him the most popular figure. At one extreme, the pinnacle of the luxury market represented by those extraordinary houses was a very small place, occupied by very few prospective clients; at the other, fame, that modern popularity built on the *opinion* expressed in the illustrated press, in cartoons or on postcards (hundreds of different postcards of Gaudí's work appeared during his lifetime), was astonishingly extensive. Gaudí occupied both ends of the arc, the bow tensed by Madame Fashion, thanks to his intractable genius, and also at the expense of his rivals: the Batlló house undoubtedly marks the moment of his triumph.

Before then, not coincidentally, Gaudí had, as we know, won the City Council's first competition with the Calvet house [fig. 100], and when he built the Palau Güell [fig. 75, 101, 102, 143] the press had hailed his extraordinary originality, specifically emphasizing the fact that the virtues of both the architect and the client—or, better, the patron—were reflected in that mansion. In 1894, for example, Josep Puiggarí wrote with reference to Gaudí and Güell that 'an artist, a man truly worthy of the great name must possess something essentially *sui generis*, thanks to which he is himself and not another', and in 1890 Frederic Rahola had stressed that the main reason for the success of the Palau Güell was that Eusebi Güell had 'allowed the artist to move, with complete freedom, having full confidence in his talent, without worrying about the excommunications of the vulgar'.[35]

Gaudí is the artist, 'a true eccentric,' Rahola writes; it is not surprising that years later Francesc Pujols should have ranked him among the architects of Barcelona —who are very few: three—in first place. Nor that Gaudí's work should be seen as a constant challenge to and always *in discord* with itself: an internal rivalry that was also, without paradox, absolutely extroverted. In October 1909 Apa published a cartoon in *Papitu* entitled 'Strong Houses' [fig. 105]. This shows two men —one of them is Pere Falqués, the architect who designed the Passeig de Gràcia street lights [fig. 83]—in front of the Milà house, then under construction [fig. 106]. 'Which house do you like best, Mr Falqués: this one for Milà, the Batlló house, the Güell house, the Calvet house ...?'. Falqués's response—'the Ballarín house'—[36] is irrelevant now. The important thing is the impressive list of works and that *public* question: Which do you like best? Like the pictures at a modern exhibition, *l'art dans la rue*: it is *eccentricity* that must continually surpass itself.

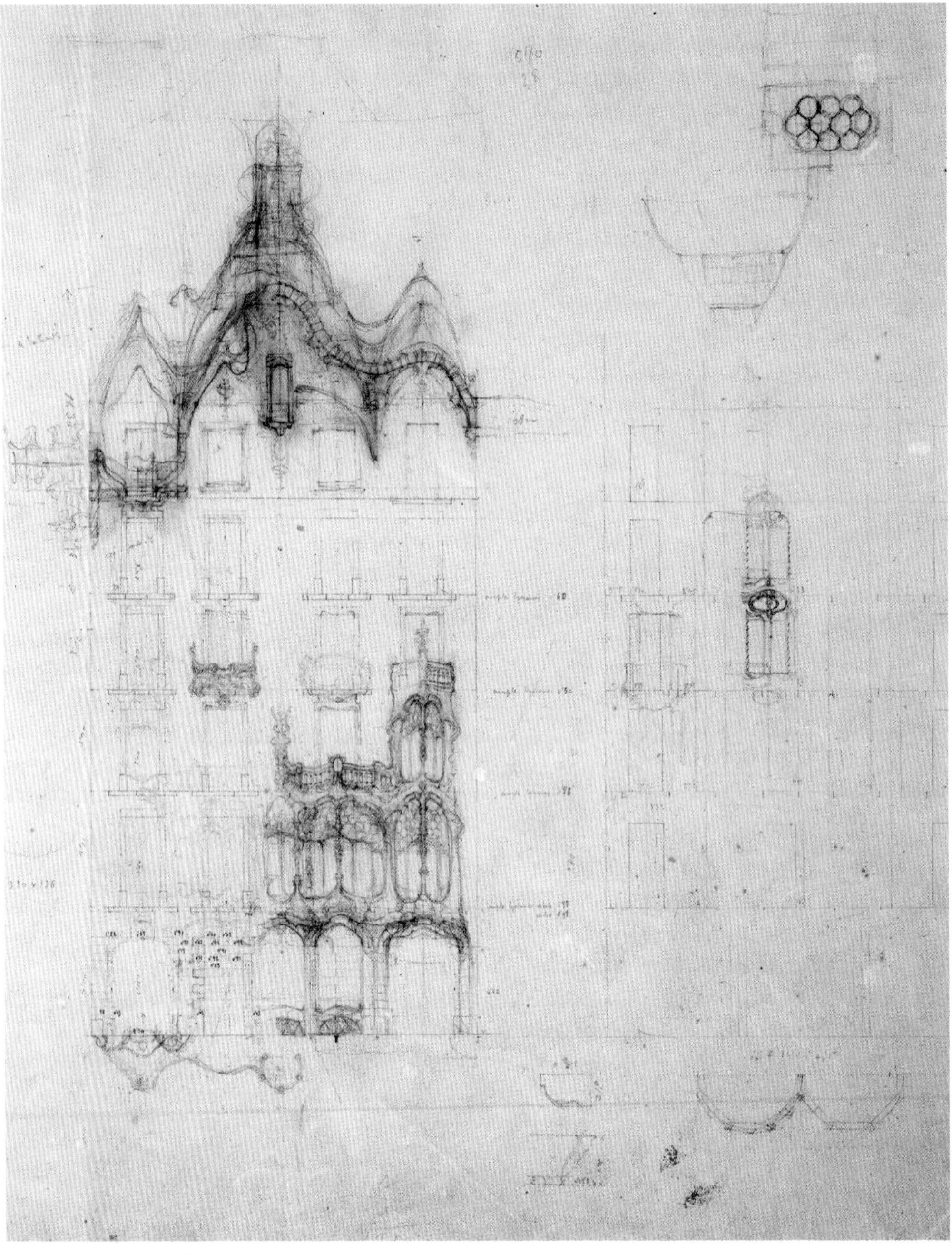

fig. 98, following page fig. 99

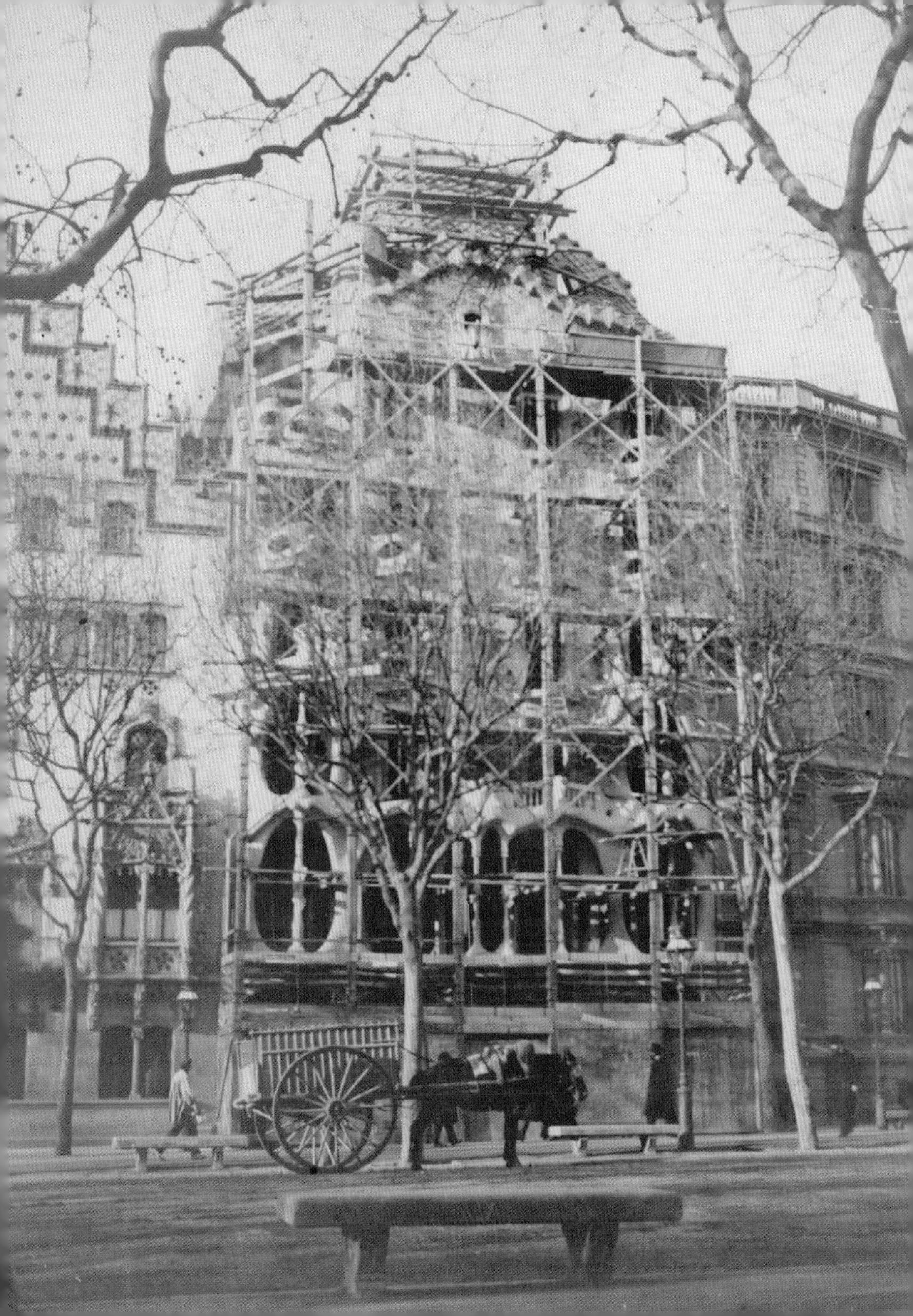

fig. 100, 101, 102

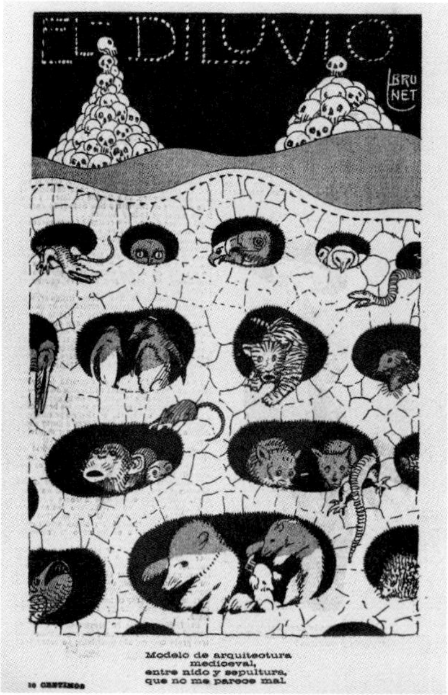

fig. 103, 104, 105, 106

There is no doubt that, in the end, the Milà house [fig. 108-115] was the culmination of that race: built on a chamfered corner, on an exceptionally large plot by the usual standards of the Eixample, and beset by controversies and lawsuits, it was more caricatured, more photographed [fig. 109, 111, 113-115] and was from the outset more visited by tourists than the Batlló house. But it was here, as we have seen, that Gaudí's *popularity*, that form of success specific to modern society, was definitively established: more open and immediate than the Palau Güell [fig. 101, 102]; built, unlike the outlying Sagrada Família and the even more distant Park Güell, both then unfinished, in the very centre of the city; more extravagant and fantastical than the Calvet house, and, ultimately, to say it with propriety, more commercial than any of his previous works, the Batlló house was also probably the first in which the public—that new judge—was truly aware of correspondence between Gaudí's strategy as an artist and the excess of his forms, in which originality or imagination are presented as figures of overconsumption.

At the Universal Exposition in Paris in 1900, when architecture in the *modern style*, as the scenario of the largest concentration of crowds and goods ever seen, triumphed and at the same time was execrated by the serious press and ridiculed by the satirical press, the old metaphor of the pâtisserie—supreme trope of the overconsumption we are talking about— was more popular than ever. In April 1900, for example, in *Le Figaro*, Caran d'Ache (Emmanuel Poiré) published a cartoon, 'Le cordon bleu', depicting the interior of a kitchen with a huge cake on the counter, made up of the succession of strangely shaped arches, domes and towers of the Exposition buildings [fig. 119].[37] Many years later, in 1933, when Salvador Dalí was drafting his famous article 'De la beauté térrifiante et comestible de l'architecture Modern'Style (Of the Terrifying and Edible Beauty of Art Nouveau Architecture) [fig. 107] and referred to *Modernisme* in general and the work of Gaudí in particular as 'la pâtisserie Barcelone', his use of the expression merely confirmed the stubborn persistence of the metaphor in specific relation to that architecture and thus the continuance of its extraordinary success.[38]

I suspect that, like other trades related to bourgeois luxury consumption—such as art or architecture—the pastry shops must have known great times at the turn of the twentieth century. Can we forget that in *The Bible of Amiens*, which we mentioned in the previous chapter, Ruskin himself suggests that visitors to the cathedral should stop in rue des Trois Cailloux on their way up from the railway station and 'get into a cheerful temper' by buying 'some bonbons or tarts for the children in one of the charming patissier's shops to the left'?[39]

following pages, fig. 107

DE LA BEAUTÉ TERRIFIANTE ET COMESTIBLE, DE L'ARCHITECTURE MODERN' STYLE.

par

SALVADOR DALI

INCOMPRÉHENSION COLOSSALE, RAVISSANTE DU PHÉNOMÈNE. — L'utilisation facilement littéraire du « 1900 » tend à devenir affreusement continue. On se sert pour la justifier d'une formule aimable, à succès légèrement nostalgique, légèrement comique, susceptible de provoquer une « espèce de sourire » particulièrement répugnant : il s'agit d'un discret et spirituel « Ris donc, Paillasse » basé sur les mécanismes les plus lamentables de la « perspective sentimentale » grâce auxquels il est possible de juger par contraste, avec un recul très exagéré, d'une époque relativement proche. De cette manière l'*anachronisme*, c'est-à-dire le « concret délirant » (unique constante vitale) nous est présenté (en considération de l'esthétisme intellectualiste qu'on nous prête) comme l'essence de l'« éphémère dépaysé » (ridicule - mélancolique). Il s'agit, comme on voit, d'une « attitude » basée sur le plus petit, sur le moins orgueilleux « complexe de supériorité» auquel vient s'ajouter un coefficient d'humour « sordide-critique » qui rend tout le monde content et permet, à quiconque veut montrer le souci des confites actualités artistiques-rétrospectives, d'apprécier le phénomène inouï avec les contractions faciales réglementaires et décentes. Ces contractions faciales, réflexes, traîtresses, de « refoule-défense » auront pour effet de faire alterner les sourires bénévoles et compréhensifs — teints, il est vrai, de l'indispensable larme bien connue (correspondant aux « souvenirs conventionnels », simulés) — et les rires francs, explosifs, irrésistibles quoique non révélateurs de vulgarité, chaque fois qu'apparaît un de ces « anachronismes » violents, hallucinants, qu'il s'agisse d'un de ces tragiques et grandioses costumes sado-masochistes-comestibles ou, plus paradoxalement encore, d'une de ces terrifiantes et sublîmes architectures ornementales du Modern' Style.

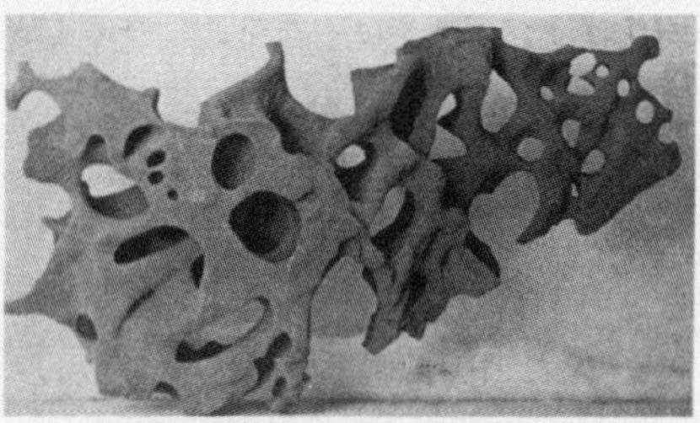

ESSAI DE MODERN'STYLE GÉOLOGIQUE, RATÉ COMME TOUT CE QUI VIENT DE LA NATURE PRIVÉE D'IMAGINATION.

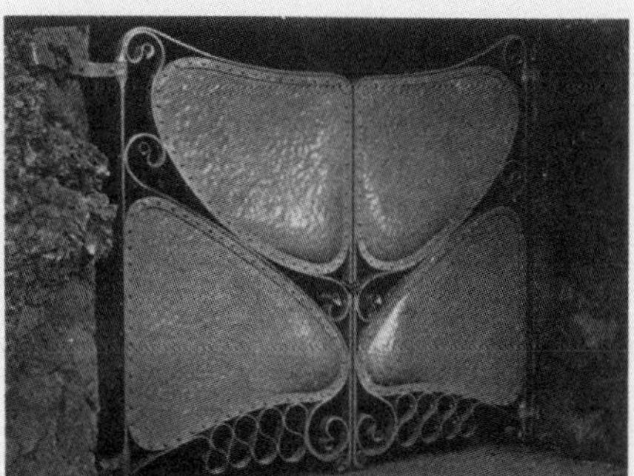

ON PÉNÈTRE DANS LES GROTTES PAR DE TENDRES PORTES EN FOIE DE VEAU.

LES VAGUES FOSSILES DE LA MER...

Je crois avoir été le premier en 1929 et au début de *La Femme visible*, à considérer, sans l'ombre d'humour, l'architecture délirante du Modern'Style comme le phénomène le plus original et le plus extraordinaire de l'histoire de l'art.

J'insiste ici sur le caractère essentiellement *extra-plastique du Modern'Style*. Toute utilisation de celui-ci à des fins proprement « plastiques » ou picturales ne manquerait pas d'impliquer pour moi la trahison la plus flagrante des aspirations irrationalistes et essentiellement « littéraires de ce mouvement. Le « remplacement » (question de fatigue) de la formule « angle droit » et « section d'or » par la formule convulsive-ondulante ne peut à la longue que donner naissance à un esthétisme aussi triste que le précédent — moins ennuyeux momentanément à cause du changement, c'est tout. Les meilleurs se réclament de cette formule : la ligne courbe paraît redevenir aujourd'hui le plus court chemin d'un point à un autre, le plus vertigineux, — mais tout cela n'est que la « misère dernière du plasticisme ». Décorativisme antidécoratif, contraire au décorativisme psychique du Modern'Style.

★

APPARITION DE L'IMPÉRIALISME CANNIBALE DU MODERN' STYLE. — Les causes « manifestes » de production du Modern' Style nous apparaissent encore trop confuses, trop contradictoires et trop vastes pour qu'il soit question d'en trancher dans l'actualité. On pourrait en dire autant de ses causes « latentes » bien que le lecteur intelligent puisse être amené à déduire de ce qui va être dit que le mouvement qui nous occupe a eu surtout pour but d'éveiller une sorte de grande « faim originale ».

LES OS SONT

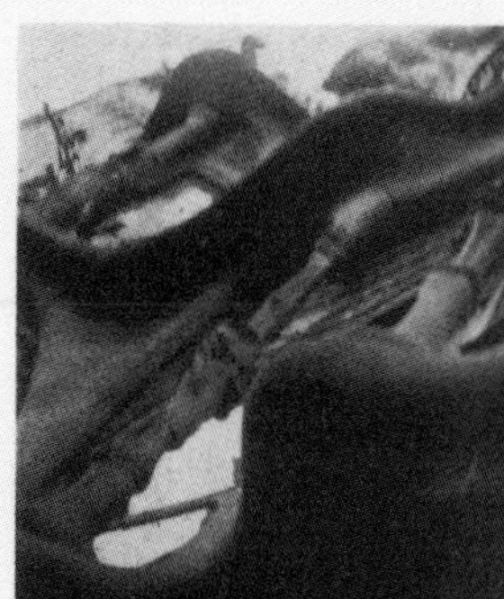

De même que la détermination de ses causes « phénoménologiques », toute entreprise de mise au point historique en ce qui

ET L'ÉCUME EN FER FORGÉ. *Man Ray.*

le concerne se heurterait aux plus grandes difficultés, et ceci surtout en raison de ce contradictoire et rare *sentiment collectif d'individualisme féroce* qui caractérise sa genèse. Bornons-nous donc à constater uniquement, aujourd'hui, le « fait » de l'apparition brusque, de l'irruption violente du Modern' Style, témoignant d'une révolution sans précédent du« sentiment d'originalité ». Le Modern' Style se présente en effet comme un bond, avec tout ce que celui-ci peut entraîner de plus cruels traumatismes pour l'art.

A L'EXTÉRIEUR.

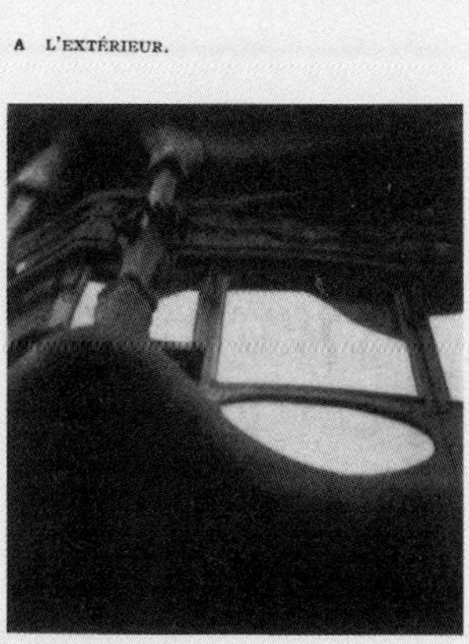

C'est dans l'architecture que nous allons pouvoir admirer l'ébranlement profond, dans son essence la plus consubstantiellement fonctionnaliste, de tout «élément », fût-il le plus congénital, le plus héréditaire du passé. Avec le Modern' Style les éléments architecturaux du passé, outre qu'ils vont être soumis à la fréquente, à la totale trituration convulsive-formelle qui va donner naissance à une nouvelle stylisation, seront appelés à revivre, à subsister couramment sous leur véritable aspect originaire, de sorte qu'en se combinant les uns avec les autres, en se fondant les uns dans les autres (en dépit de leurs antagonismes intellectuellement les plus irréconciliables, les plus irréductibles) ils vont atteindre au plus haut degré de dépréciation esthétique, manifester dans leurs rapports cette affreuse impureté qui n'a d'équivalente et d'égale que la pureté immaculée des entrelacement oniriques.

Dans un bâtiment modern' style, le gothique se métamorphose en hellénique, en extrême-oriental, et, pour peu que cela passe par la tête — par une certaine fantaisie involontaire — en Renaissance qui peut à son tour devenir modern' style pur, dynamique-asymétrique (!) tout cela dans le temps et dans l'espace « débile » d'*une seule fenêtre*, c'est-à-dire dans ce temps et cet espace peu connus et vraisemblablement vertigineux qui, comme nous venons de l'insinuer, ne seraient autres que ceux du rêve. Tout ce qui a été le plus naturellement utilitaire et

A. T. V. — 2049 - BARCELONA
Construcciones modernas. Paseo de Gracia. num. 92
Arquitecto : D. Antonio Gaudí

fig. 108, 109

—Papà, papà, jo vuy una *mona* grossa com aquesta.

fig. 110, 111

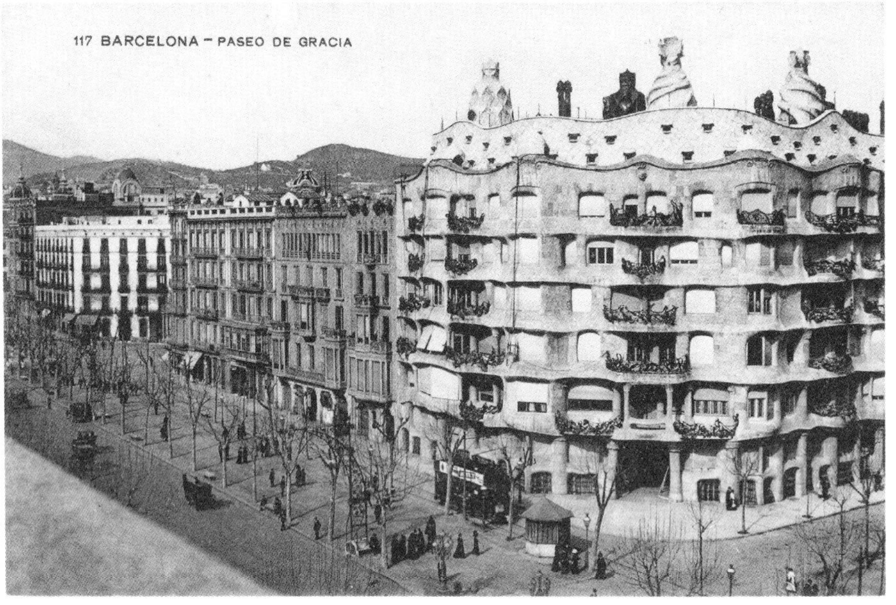
117 BARCELONA – PASEO DE GRACIA

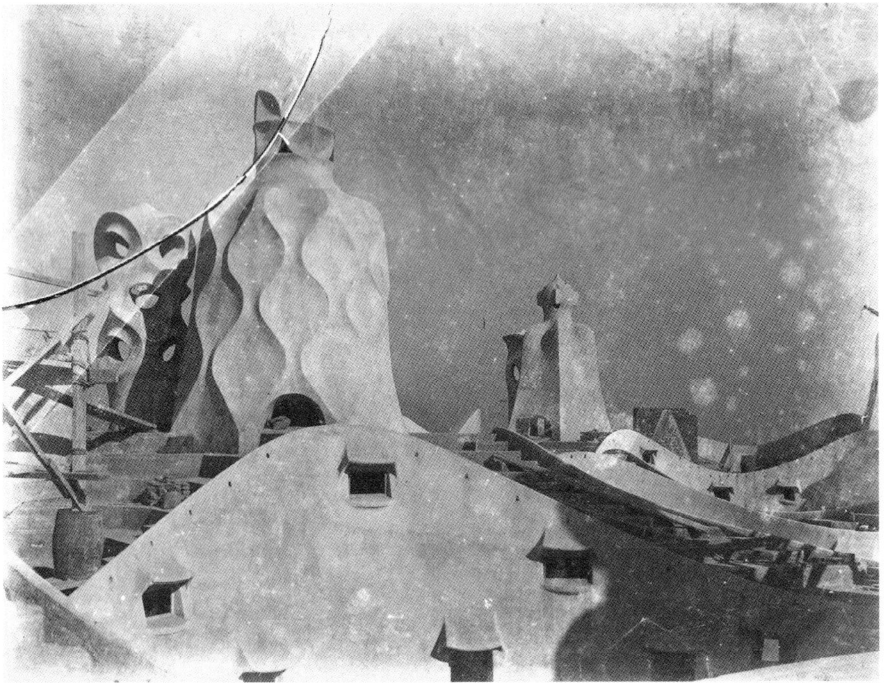

fig. 112, 113

fig. 114, 115

—Vaja, sembla que això de tallar els arbres ho fassin expressament pera que certs arquitectes ensenyin les vergonyes.

fig. 116, 117, 118, following page fig. 119

LE CORDON BLEU

PAR CARAN D'ACHE

— On peut se mettre à table!

NOTES D'UN PARISIEN

Tous les jours, on fonde quelque banquet nouveau. Je lisais hier que les anciens secrétaires de la Chambre des députés ont organisé, eux aussi, un dîner commémoratif. Pourquoi pas? On se réunit bien entre anciens camarades de collège. On peut bien se revoir aussi, si l'on me passe le mot, entre anciens camarades de collège... électoral. Tout le monde, dans sa vie, a été plus ou moins secrétaire de quelque chose. C'est un des privilèges en même temps qu'une des corvées de la jeunesse.

Mais l'on a bientôt fait de passer ce grade-là. Les secrétaires d'âge de la Chambre ne sont déjà plus de tout jeunes gens, puisqu'on n'est éligible qu'à vingt-cinq ans. Et ils vieillissent plus vite que partout ailleurs. Si l'on repassait la liste de tous les anciens secrétaires, on serait surpris d'y voir figurer certains noms. Qui croirait, par exemple, que le respectable M. Sarrien a occupé ces juvéniles fonctions? Il figure, cependant, en tête des organisateurs de ce banquet.

Il est vrai que dès la première réunion, on s'est empressé de le nommer président. On commence par être secrétaire, on finit par être doyen. Et c'est pourquoi, je le crains bien, ce dîner aura la mélancolie de tant d'autres qui lui ressemblent. On n'a que trop sujet de se voir vieillir. Pourquoi multiplier ces occasions-là? A moins que ce ne soit pour constater que les années n'épargnent pas plus les camarades que vous-même, et pour se consoler par le mot si « humain » de M. de Tillancourt disant d'un de ses anciens collègues qu'il retrouvait au Parlement, après l'avoir perdu de vue depuis plus de vingt ans:

— Ce pauvre Untel, il est tellement changé qu'il ne me reconnaissait plus!...

E.

STATISTIQUE INTÉRESSANTE

LA DÉFAITE DE RABAH

Il y a trois jours, en annonçant l'heureuse concentration sur les bords du Tchad des trois missions qui avaient pris pour objectif de leurs efforts le grand lac africain, nous disions combien la mission Gentil avait facilité la tâche des autres missions en infligeant à Rabah, le 29 octobre dernier, la sanglante défaite qui devait transformer en vaincu et en fugitif le chef noir en qui l'on voyait déjà un nouveau Samory.

Sur ce combat, nous ne possédions encore que quelques renseignements peu détaillés, venus par des télégrammes forcément concis. Le dernier courrier de la côte occidentale d'Afrique vient d'apporter au ministère des colonies un rapport complet de M. Gentil, et nous savons ainsi que nos troupes coloniales ont remporté dans cette journée un succès qui est grandement à leur honneur.

Rappelons sommairement les faits:

A la suite du massacre de l'administrateur Bretonnet, massacre qui eut lieu le 17 juillet, M. Gentil se résolut à attaquer Rabah dans sa position de Kouno, où il s'était solidement établi et de laquelle il tentait de reprendre les hostilités contre notre protégé le sultan du Baghirmi et contre nos postes du Haut-Chari.

Toutes les forces disponibles du Chari se trouvaient concentrées à Fort-Archambault, camp retranché bâti par nos troupes, par 9° 15' de latitude Nord environ, sur la rive gauche du fleuve. La marche en avant fut préparée du 17 au 23 octobre. Le commandement supérieur des troupes fut confié à M. le capitaine Robillot, qui disposait des forces suivantes:

1° La flottille, composée de la chaloupe-canonnière le *Léon-Blot*, armée d'un canon à tir rapide, d'un chaland accouplé au *Léon-Blot* et armé d'un canon-revolver, de deux boats en acier et d'une embarcation en bois. Le tout servi par un personnel de 2 Européens et de 45 indigènes, dont 25 combattants.

2° L'artillerie comprenant une section de 80 m/m de montagne et une section de 65 m/m de la marine et servie par 3 Européens.

3° Trois compagnies de tirailleurs auxiliaires à effectif réduit, comprenant: l'une 3 Européens et 127 indigènes, l'autre 3 Européens et 97 indigènes, la troisième 3 Européens et 83 indigènes. C'était, au total, un effectif de 344 combattants indigènes et 20 Européens. Tandis qu'une vingtaine d'hommes étaient laissés à Fort-Archambault, sous les ordres d'un maréchal des logis, tout le reste, c'est-à-dire les trois compagnies Julien, de Cointel et Lamothe, fut désigné pour la marche en avant.

M. le capitaine Robillot donne le récit suivant du combat, au cours d'un rapport en date du 8 novembre 1899:

Le départ de Fort-Archambault eut lieu le 23 octobre, au point du jour. Les trois compagnies devaient suivre la rive gauche du fleuve parallèlement à la flottille, de façon que les deux groupes pussent se prêter mutuellement appui. La flottille devait, chaque soir, alimenter la colonne de terre en vivres et lui faire franchir les affluents sur les bras du Chari qu'elle rencontrerait. La marche jusqu'à Kouno s'effectua de cette manière. Toutefois, le grand nombre d'affluents des bras latéraux du Chari et les immenses marais qui le bordent rendaient la marche sensiblement pénible. La colonne de terre était parfois obligée de s'écarter beaucoup de la rive. Jusqu'à 10 kilomètres en amont du Niellim, atteint le 27 au soir, les deux groupes n'ont pu se réunir que trois fois en sept jours.

Le 28, après un dernier passage de marigot, les deux groupes campaient à 4 kilomètres de Kouno. La marche n'a présenté aucune espèce d'incident. On marchait de cinq heures du matin à cinq heures du soir, avec deux heures de grand'halte — de onze heures à une heure — à raison de 2 kilomètres à 2 kilomètres 1/2 à l'heure, presque toujours sans chemin frayé. Les indigènes avaient déserté le pays. La colonne n'entra en relation avec eux qu'un peu avant le défilé de Niellim, où elle fut rejointe par des envoyés de Gaourang, et aux montagnes même, où les habitants nous firent fête et nous confirmèrent les nouvelles suivantes: « Rabah est à Kouno et ne croit pas à l'arrivée des Français. Une partie de ses forces est sur le Logone, devant Laï. Beaucoup de ses guerriers cernent le pays, en quête de vivres. »

Le 29 au matin, après une nuit absolument calme, pendant laquelle nos patrouilles constatent que les groupes des cases entourant Kouno sont encore habitées, la marche est reprise sur le camp de Rabah. A trois kilomètres de la ville, l'artillerie est débarquée en arrière des derniers mouvements de terrain et traînée à bras au centre de la colonne qui suit exactement la berge, les trois compagnies en échiquier. Le service des munitions est assuré par les non-combattants de la flottille et les porteurs, qui ont échangé leurs charges contre des caisses de projectiles. L'artillerie a, de cette manière, quarante charges de munition avec les pièces. Aussitôt ce débarquement opéré, la flottille reprend le large et se maintient à hauteur de l'avant-garde. Une série de signaux convenus d'avance, la met en liaison avec la colonne de terre.

A deux kilomètres de Kouno, au moment où elle sort des derniers fourrés, la colonne se trouve en présence d'une mince ligne de tirailleurs ennemis. Ils sont à cinq cents mètres environ des premières cases de la ville et avancent rapidement. En arrière de ceux-ci, on aperçoit des groupes plus nombreux sortir de la ville et entamer un mouvement tournant sur la gauche de la colonne. Presque immédiatement, l'artillerie de la colonne de terre et celle de la flottille ouvrent simultanément le feu sur les plus grandes masses ennemies et sur la ville. Rabah répond avec les trois pièces de 4, prises aux Baghirmiens, dont le tir, admirablement réglé en trois coups, nous cause des pertes sérieuses toute la journée. Le combat, commencé à neuf heures trente du matin, se prolonge, en avançant lentement jusqu'à six cents mètres de la ville, jusque vers onze heures et demie. A cette heure, et au moment où la droite ennemie commence à se rabattre sur le derrière de la colonne, celle-ci se porte brusquement en avant, culbute toute la gauche ennemie, qui entraîne dans sa retraite le reste de l'armée de Rabah, et enlève la ville que les tirailleurs incendient en avançant.

Malheureusement, emportées par leur élan, les deux premières compagnies se jettent sur le camp fortifié, construit au centre de la ville, d'où part un feu des plus violents. En un instant, elles sont décimées, le maréchal des logis de Possel est tué au moment où il tente d'escalader le réduit. Les deux compagnies sont forcées de reculer de quelques mètres et viennent s'abriter derrière les cases les plus rapprochées du réduit. Elles sont rapidement remises en ordre.

A partir de ce moment, l'action se concentre exclusivement sur le saillant du réduit, où nous nous efforçons d'ouvrir une brèche, pendant qu'à travers la palissade les tirailleurs criblent de balles les derniers défenseurs de la ville. Le combat est, de part et d'autre, extrêmement meurtrier; l'artillerie ennemie éteint son feu vers trois heures; mais, une demi-heure plus tard, la nôtre, qui s'est avancée jusqu'à 50 mètres du réduit, n'a plus qu'une pièce en état de servir, et bientôt ses munitions sont épuisées sans que la brèche ait été ouverte.

A ce moment, Rabah, battu en plaine, est en fuite depuis midi avec presque toute son armée, ses pertes sont énormes et il ne reste dans le réduit que quelques défenseurs qui se feront tuer jusqu'au dernier pour protéger la retraite de leur maître, en nous infligeant des pertes irréparables.

De notre côté, nous avons près de moitié de l'effectif hors de combat, et l'assaut du réduit, qui n'est plus qu'un charnier et sera forcément évacué la nuit, nous coûterait le reste de nos tirailleurs. Aussi, malgré leur désir de tenter l'escalade, je donne l'ordre, à quatre heures, d'incendier la ville et de se replier au bord du Chari, à l'accotage de la flottille. Celle-ci est mouillée à 1,200 mètres du fort de Kouno, sur un banc de sable complètement nu, où toute surprise de nuit est impossible, si l'ennemi était encore à même d'en tenter une.

La retraite s'opère par échelons, dans l'ordre le plus parfait, les blessés, les armes et les munitions ramassés au fur et à mesure par l'échelon qui rompt le premier, pendant que les autres battent le réduit et les cases de feux de salve qui empêchent les défenseurs de tenter tout retour offensif.

A six heures, les trois compagnies avaient rallié le *Léon-Blot* sans être poursuivies. Le combat était terminé.

Les troupes campaient devant la ville, protégées par une petite tranchée-abri faite en quelques minutes dans le sable, et les hommes, harassés, pouvaient enfin manger et prendre un peu de repos.

Pendant l'action et sous le feu de l'ennemi, tous les blessés avaient été pansés. La flottille avait largement contribué au succès de la journée: 1° en bombardant la ville et les réserves ennemies; 2° en poursuivant en aval de Kouno des bandes qui fuyaient le long des rives; enfin, en assurant pendant toute la journée, avec une régularité parfaite, le ravitaillement en cartouches et en munitions d'artillerie.

Le combat de Kouno nous coûte: un maréchal des logis tué, le maréchal des logis Possel; 40 indigènes tués, 4 Européens blessés.

Le 30 au matin, aucune démonstration hostile de l'ennemi ne s'est produite. Kouno est décidément évacué. Le retour à Fort-Archambault est décidé; il s'opère par la rive droite du fleuve, qui offre une route plus facile, et le 5 novembre, toute la colonne était de retour au fort.

Les résultats de ce combat sont considérables, le but fixé a été pleinement atteint. Nos morts de Niellim sont victorieusement vengés et les pertes de Rabah sont énormes. Quant à lui, vaincu pour la première fois à son camp, puis chassé de la ville qu'il avait construite et qui a été incendiée sous ses yeux, forcé de fuir précipitamment, il a dû se replier sur Dikoa, capitale du Cobala, abandonnant le territoire du Baghirmi. Son prestige est fortement ébranlé et ses soldats, déjà très éprouvés par le combat de Niellim, semblent complètement découragés. Enfin, la retraite de Rabah, entraînant celle de ses lieutenants, a permis au sultan Gaourang de nous faire parvenir des alliés aussitôt après notre retour au Fort-Archambault. Sa jonction avec nous n'est plus qu'une question de jours.

Le rapport de M. le capitaine Robillot se termine par des détails sur la tactique, l'artillerie et les fortifications de Rabah. Ces détails sont fort intéressants, en ce qu'ils montrent que l'armée de Rabah méritait bien le nom d'armée, et que, pour en triompher, il a fallu toute l'habileté et toute la vaillance de nos troupes:

Les soldats de Rabah étaient tous armés de fusils, la plupart à tir rapide. Ils ont un certain nombre de fusils du calibre Lebel, entre les mains des meilleurs tireurs. Beaucoup de cartouches sont refaites et ont perdu une partie de leurs qualités. Les anciens étuis sont réamorcés avec une capsule Gévelot coupée perpendiculairement à son axe et dans laquelle une perle Bagaka tient lieu d'enclume. La capsule est maintenue au centre de la cartouche par de la cire d'abeilles. Les balles refaites par Rabah sont en étain, de la forme de la balle du fusil Gras 74, mal ébarbées et produisant de vilaines blessures; mais elles sont trop légères, mal calibrées, et ont par suite peu de portée.

Les canonniers ont été bien instruits, par des gens capables de bien diriger un tir d'artillerie. Celui-ci a été réglé en trois coups, et nous aurions souffert énormément si la nature sablonneuse du terrain n'avait empêché beaucoup d'obus d'éclater.

Les soldats de Rabah sont d'excellents tirailleurs, tirant juste et se servant très bien du terrain, ils forcent leur ennemi à prendre de suite des formations minces, peu vulnérables, qui constitueraient un danger s'ils profitaient ensuite de leur énorme supériorité numérique ou de leur cavalerie pour attaquer.

Mais s'ils ont un sentiment d'offensive par le feu très marqué, ils manquent d'élan, la confiance dans leurs fusils leur a fait abandonner les armes blanches, ils sont incapables de résister à une attaque à la baïonnette. Si la colonne avait disposé de cavalerie, le combat de Kouno se serait changé pour Rabah en un véritable désastre.

Le réduit de Kouno avait la forme d'un rectangle, terminé en éperon sur une de ses faces et partagé en deux compartiments. La capitale du saillant est orientée à peu près vers N.-E., la pointe vers le fleuve. Les défenseurs tirent par le bas de la palissade; à certains endroits, les cases intérieures du tata forment un double étage de feu, des tireurs placés dans les arbres en forment un troisième.

La ville était placée au milieu d'un bois de haute futaie, le réduit noyé au milieu de cases.

Si cette disposition permet à l'infanterie d'approcher très près de l'ouvrage, elle a l'inconvénient de masquer complètement les fortifications au feu de l'artillerie qui est forcée de s'approcher beaucoup trop. Le tir à grande distance était arrêté par les arbres et les projectiles éclataient dans les branches, 200 ou 300 mètres avant d'arriver dans le réduit.

A ce récit du capitaine Robillot, il convient d'ajouter le passage suivant, extrait du rapport de M. le commissaire Gentil, confirmant sur les autres points les détails donnés par le commandant des forces dans le Chari:

J'ai assisté à l'action et j'en ai suivi toutes les phases. Le rapport du capitaine Robillot les relate avec la plus grande fidélité. Il n'a omis qu'une chose, c'est de parler de lui, c'est-à-dire que blessé, à trois heures et demie, et perdant des flots de sang, il n'a cessé de diriger le combat avec le même calme et le même sang-froid. Je ne veux pas apprécier les admirables qualités militaires du capitaine Robillot; d'autres plus qualifiés que moi, entre autres le colonel Combes, qui se connaissait en hommes, se sont chargés de ce soin. Mais j'insiste d'une façon spéciale sur la valeur de M. Robillot, au point de vue politique et administratif.

Le combat de Kouno restera un titre de gloire pour ceux qui y ont pris part. Il montre que le pays peut avoir la même confiance en ses enfants que par le passé.

L'affaire de Kouno se termine donc par la destruction complète de cette place; des chevaux, des bœufs ont été brûlés dans les écuries, ainsi que tout le contenu des maisons que, dans leur certitude de vaincre, les gens de Rabah n'avaient pas déménagées.

Rabah, pour la première fois vaincu depuis de nombreuses années, a perdu une partie de son prestige.

Tels sont les détails qui sont parvenus au ministère des colonies. Sans doute Rabah, ayant réussi à échapper à nos coups, peut peut-être trouver des partisans et nous susciter un jour ou l'autre de nouvelles difficultés. Mais c'est surtout en Afrique que l'autorité d'un chef ne survit pas à une défaite. Le vaincu de Kouno aura de la peine, malgré tout, à voir son étoile luire de nouveau. Et si nous avons la sagesse de maintenir dans ces régions des forces convenables, il ne sera guère à craindre. L'accès du Tchad par le Chari nous est désormais acquis.

M. L.

AU PAYS D'ALPHONSE DAUDET

PAR DÉPÊCHE DE NOTRE ENVOYÉ SPÉCIAL

Nîmes, 8 avril.

Par grande vitesse, cette nuit, la statue d'Alphonse Daudet est arrivée. Des travailleurs nocturnes l'ont placée sur un socle très bas, au milieu d'un bassin, dans un square où se balancent six peupliers énormes.

L'endroit est assez mal choisi. Ce morceau de jardin municipal, étriqué entre les murailles voisines, eût peut-être convenu au monument de quelque philosophe austère. Il sied mal à celui dont le génie était fait de mouvement et de soleil. On semble avoir mesuré l'espace à celui qui n'aimait que les larges horizons, la lumière à celui dont l'âme était éprise de couleurs.

Et je m'explique pourquoi Falguière a livré avec quelque regret son œuvre et pourquoi son dernier coup de pouce d'artiste n'a pas encore été donné. Tout à l'heure, quand les discours officiels salueront le marbre du maître, on ne le verra pas sur l'estrade d'honneur parmi les chamarrures et les galas, mais caché derrière un rideau de sa chambre, à l'hôtel qui touche au square. Il attendra avec quelque impatience que la cérémonie soit achevée.

— Je vous ai prêté ma statue, me disait-il hier, dès demain je la remporte.

Et le grand sculpteur fera bien de reprendre son œuvre. Non pas certes qu'elle ne soit une belle chose, mais Falguière ne nous a pas représenté Alphonse Daudet tel que l'avenir le comprendra. Il l'a fait mélancolique, presque douloureux; il lui a donné une allure grave et songeuse. Cet homme que nous voyons là, accoudé sur une roche, la tête penchée, tenant la plume d'une main alanguie, n'est pas le Daudet qui fit ce poème de joie: *Tartarin*, qui nous donna ce bouquet de parfums et de rayons: *Les lettres de mon moulin*. L'artiste a fait sortir de son marbre un penseur sévère qui songe aux lourds problèmes de l'humanité. C'est là une erreur que quelques coups de ciseaux corrigeront.

Nîmes s'est quelque peu réveillée de sa torpeur maussade d'hier. C'est dimanche, le ciel est bleu et la ville semble se remuer dans du soleil et de la poussière, les cloches de Pâques fleuries carillonnent sur les toits, il y a des promeneurs dans les rues et des pompiers autour du square. Mais la foule, la grande foule qui fait les manifestations magnifiques, est absente. Elle sera tout à l'heure aux arènes pour acclamer quatre vaches et six toréadors régionaux. Mais Alphonse Daudet, compatriote illustre, ne va pas dans leur admiration à la taille de cette prima spada nîmoise Le Pouly.

Et je regrette sincèrement pour cette jolie ville, où l'art pourtant a laissé partout des traces, cette indifférence de mauvais goût. Alphonse Daudet, à qui les imbéciles seuls reprochent ses ironies et ses plaisanteries méridionales, aurait dû mettre d'accord toute la population. Devant un gloire comme celle-là, il n'aurait dû y avoir ni question politique ni question tauromachique. Si Tartarin a laissé de la famille à Nîmes, ses héritiers auraient fait leur devoir en prenant place dans le Comité du monument. Nous avons vu, au contraire, des bouderies et des rancunes. Ah! le joli livre que le maître pourra écrire dans l'autre monde s'il a des loisirs dans le paradis! Quel piquant épilogue à ses tartarinades avec l'histoire de ses compatriotes nîmois!

Malgré tout, l'inauguration du monument a été fort belle et le succès en revient pour une grande partie à un journaliste de talent qui fut l'ami de Daudet et défend ici sa mémoire, notre confrère Paul Guiraud. Des trois discours qui ont salué la statue du maître, il en est un qu'il faudra lire dans son texte, car c'est une belle page de style, de pensées et de sentiments. M. Henri Roujon, directeur des Beaux-Arts, a parlé d'Alphonse Daudet en lettré, en artiste, et ce ne sont, hélas! que des extraits que je puis donner ici:

..... Au lendemain des deuils de la patrie, nous retrouvons Alphonse Daudet, frémissant encore mais ennobli et virilisé, contemplant les hommes et les choses de cet œil voilé et profond qui semblait ne rien regarder et savait tout voir. Le pur artiste renonçait à l'aimable gloire, pour lui trop facile, que lui promettaient les anthologistes. Il devenait en silence un créateur d'âmes. Un austère logis

With materials as fluid and malleable as sugar, cream, custard and chocolate, and with cherries for finishing touches, as brilliant as gemstones, *fin-de-siècle* confectioners created, as they still do today, these great masses, these stepped pyramids and fairy-tale castles, which constituted, in the shop window or on the table, a temptation first for the eyes and then for all the senses, as well as being in their gluttonous impermanence, the ultimate culmination of the idea of consumption in its most radical and truly cannibal form. No wonder, then, that delirious desire should determine that what the hungry children in the forest find will be not juicy sausages, nor an abundance of fruit, but a whole cottage of gingerbread, chocolate and candy. Nor that in the equally delirious showcases of 1900s bourgeois desire, at the Paris Exposition or on the Passeig de Gràcia [fig. 120], seeing the way the architects deformed materials, stripping them of all their tectonic qualities, their contemporaries should have used in referring to those buildings of pastry —as Francis Carco was still saying of the Milà house in 1929,[40] at which a child in a 1910 cartoon by Junceda points and exclaims 'Daddy, Daddy, I want an Easter cake as big as this one'—the metaphor of the cake shop [fig. 110].[41]

The image is not at all soft and sweet, as nice as a cake. On the contrary, it is scornful and cruel, and comes from an anonymous and desiring public's intuition that architecture has become just another product among the products on display in the market. In fact, that *elevation* of architecture to the level of the patissier's shop contains within it the perception of an obscenity: the obscenity implicit in architecture's need to make a show of its independence and its traditional strengths before the eyes of all in order to occupy its privileged place in the new shop windows of bourgeois representation, where *firmitas* and *utilitas* are no longer necessary qualities and *venustas* has been reduced to the subjectivity of an intrinsically eccentric taste.

No other architect took to such an extreme as Gaudí did the condition that the market imposes on every product that circulates in it: that it be a convincing demonstration that anything is possible. Once again a cartoon, this time by Cornet, in *Cu-Cut!* in 1912, takes the Batlló house as a paradigm of the situations we are discussing [fig. 116, 117]. Between the stumps of two felled trees, Gaudí's house, reversed but perfectly recognizable, has been turned into a quivering mass of trifle or jelly that spills over at the sides to cover the neighbouring houses; the lintels are of cream and the cornices sugar piping; the tower and chimneys are ice-cream cones and the roof chocolate flakes. A man with a cane gestures towards it and exclaims: 'Well, it seems that all this cutting down trees is done expressly so that

fig. 120, 121

fig. 122

certain architects may expose themselves!'[42] Gaudí was undoubtedly the butt of a cartoon by Opisso, published in *Cu-Cut!* a few years earlier, in 1909, featuring an elegant Passeig de Gràcia [fig. 121]: 'She: "Such a shame they didn't also prune the trees on the other side! Then we should have seen the houses." He: "Oh! That's precisely the point: that they shouldn't be seen."'[43]

As Josep Carner[44] said of Gaudí, in a verse *auca* that we shall consider in due course, 'Every hour —it's so unfair!— / he displays his flair / and disturbs with a jolt / the sage and the dolt'.[45] He is, in fact, the perfectly modern architect: the inextricably eccentric and popular figure walking a tightrope stretched across the whole arc of the market. His architecture, especially from the Batlló house on,is displayed in the spotlight, with no possibility of turning back, radically: at once letting itself be seen and putting itself in danger. I know a rare photograph of 1908 [fig. 122]. A number of strange devices (they are actually prototypes of spittoons)[46] consisting of a tubular pedestal topped by a shiny globe have been placed along the Passeig de Gràcia in front of the 'block of discord' [fig. 118]. At the moment the shot was taken, people of various classes and conditions have stopped, curious, to stare at a couple of smartly dressed men—after all, the photograph was sent as a postcard to Enrique Morell, a famous Barcelona tailor—who are pressing down on the pedal at the base of two of these objects to open the globe. In the background we see the ground floors of the Amatller house and the Batlló house, whose architecture is reflected in the shining sphere. Could we ask for a better snapshot or a more sparkling metaphor for the conditions of his spectacle? Architecture is contemplated as the great curiosity reflected in the distorting mirrors of a city converted into a spectacle of merchandise.

But wasn't the universal equivalence imposed on society by merchandise the very thing that Gaudí set out to oppose, in a vicious circle as perfect as it is perverse, with his brilliant, individualistic and constantly changing work—*sui generis,* as his contemporaries said? In the bourgeois world, the artist's showily redemptive intervention turns in vicious circles. To penetrate into the private areas of the Batlló house is to situate oneself in the most spectacular of these circles: what else does Gaudí invite us to do in abandoning the open and indifferent space of the street but to venture into the deepest interior, the original beginning?

We enter through a lobby without corners or edges [fig. 123], a cave lit by an ivory light that seems to emanate from the smoothly curving walls and ceilings. The pale grey socle formed by soft-edged ceramic tiles that are almost the imprint of their

fig. 123

own remote model, as if they had been worn smooth by long erosion, leads us to the right, to the foot of the stairs and the bottom of the light well. The railing repeats, from upright to upright, the transparent profile of some of the polyps—*Tubulariae*, for example—in the books that Ernst Haeckel published, as we know, between 1899 and 1904, whose illustrations had become fashionable among *fin-de-siècle* artists.[47] We see them contract and dilate, ascending against the strong current that forms in the wave of the wooden handrail, curved in the hard iron pillar with its well-defined profiles, on whose copper-coloured corbel the iron rivets and bands seem to have turned into corals. If we look up we see the ceramics of the light well gradually deepen from the pale blue of the lower floors to the dark blue of the upper floors. Scattered among these self-coloured ceramics are the soft-edged tiles that we saw in the lobby, whose blunt points shine here and there like water droplets in which the light is dispersed. From sky blue to navy blue: we are literally sinking upward into the seabed [fig. 136, 137].

On the left, a door with a bulbous profile affords access to the Batlló family's private patio. Once again we are in the continuous, enveloping interior of a soft-walled cave. The staircase is a succession of giant vertebrae, the great backbone of a monster [fig. 125], stranded there and occupying the entire space: a dragon or a whale. The railing turns around a golden rod swathed with metal ribbons and topped by a glass ball and a crown: a lost sceptre, perhaps, but also the tentacles of some hidden creature or its splashing. After ascending the stairs, those images are reinforced in the upper lobby: bathed in the light that falls from the amorphous skylights, the wood of the handrail undulates like the meandering course of a dense, dark interior stream [fig. 124].

The seabed and caves: surely those were some of the most successful and most popular attractions at the Universal Expositions [fig. 128]? Among the *plein-air* pavilions, scattered here and there in endless variations of style, history, continents, countries and races over the boundless expanses of the Exposition, and in contrast to the panoramic views afforded by the tethered balloons, viewing platforms and towers that culminate in the complete elimination of barriers and the bird's-eye view beyond any horizon from the Eiffel Tower, these submarine grottoes allowed the exposition visitors, tired of so much transparent light and open air, to retreat into the interior, into a closed place in which to dream, in the age of Darwin and Haeckel, not only of the return to some origin—that of Man, of the species, of the Earth—but also of the return of shadows, of tinted lights, of their own bodies bathed in the close atmosphere of the aquarium.

fig. 124, 125, 126

L'AQUARIUM D'EAU DOUCE DANS LE JARDIN RÉSERVÉ

fig. 127, 128

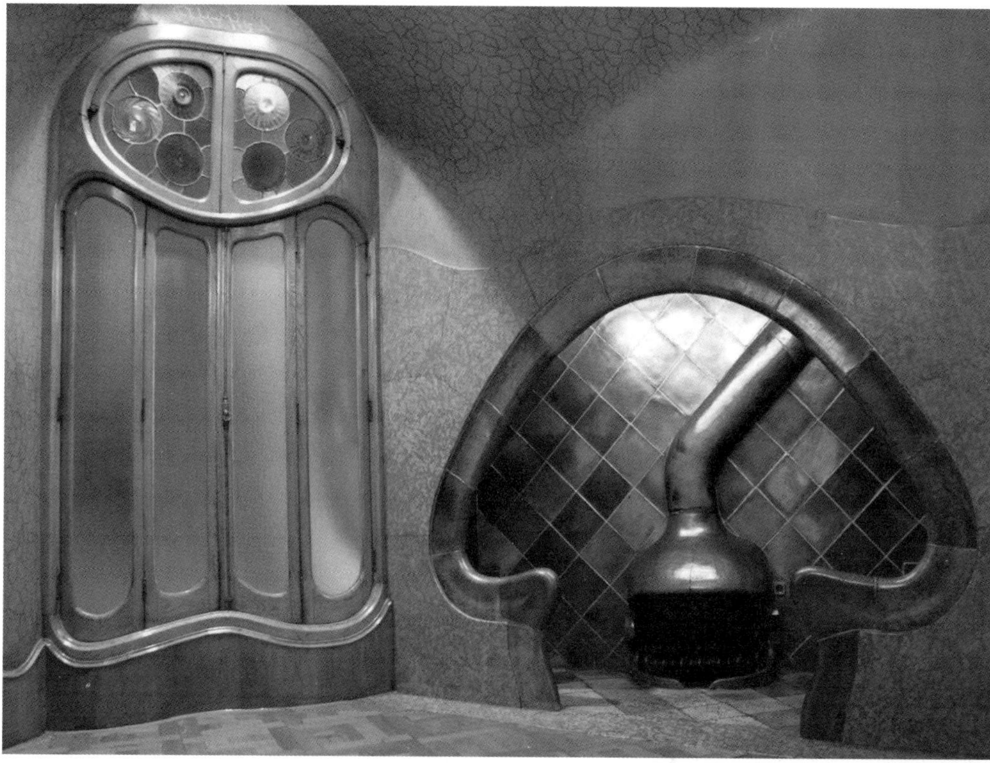

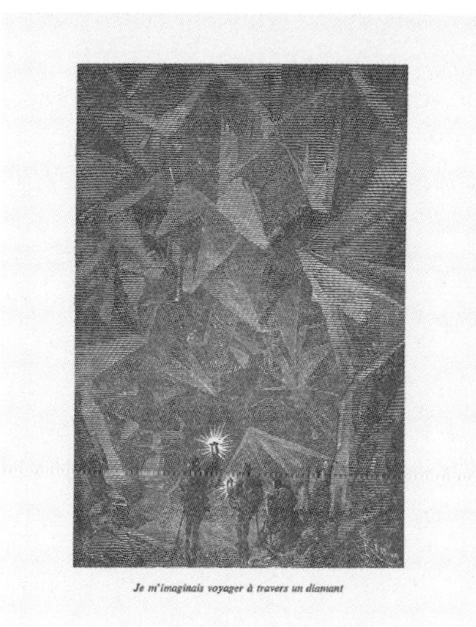
Je m'imaginais voyager à travers un diamant

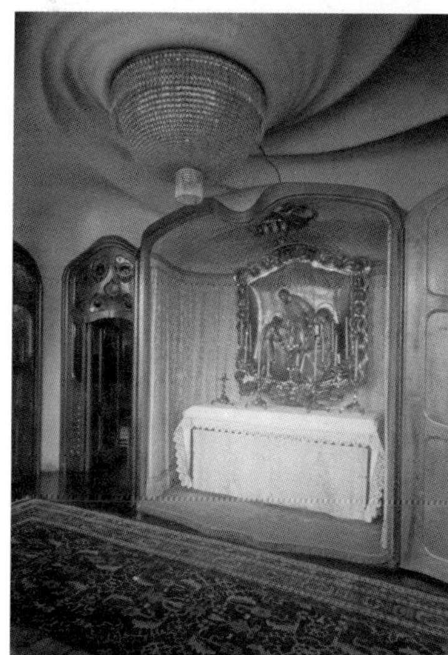

fig. 129, 130, 131

In popular epics of progress—in the novels of Jules Verne, for example—the movement of the all-conquering male, the modern hero, is always in two directions: one cosmic, toward the wide-open and unlimited distances of the new continents or outer space; the other intimate, into the cave where life is regained and protected, into the maternal womb of the earth, the primordial home from which men may spurn the out-of-control exterior that they themselves have created [fig. 130, 139]. Nature, reason and history recover their virtues in the authentic property that the cave offers and return to the origin of life in the amniotic fluid of the seabed.

The Batlló house aspires to being the underwater cave of the man who circulates among the crowds of the merchandise-city: a place in which to find himself, or at least, to find the fantasies of the *ego*. Jellyfish, corals, underground streams, antediluvian fossils: in other words this is necessarily—how could it fail to be, in *1900*!—a neurotic re-encounter, culminating in the small, soft, warm corner, cave inside the cave, of the fireplace [fig. 129]. But this is a place that takes many forms: in the softened centre of the dining room [fig. 132], for example, the ceiling condenses in the form of great drops, while the soft, almost liquid mouldings of the twin columns—inspired here, as so often, by the Patio de los Leones in the Alhambra—refer once again to extremely slow processes of erosion. On the other side, in the main lounge [fig. 134], which by way of the gallery gives onto the Passeig de Gràcia [fig. 138], the ceiling has become a vortex, the core of a whirlwind [fig. 134, 135]. Through the stained glass with its primarily greenish and bluish tones—navy, sky blue, indigo—and undulating frames, the light penetrates into these rooms of the main floor, bathing their aquatic surfaces with aquarium light [fig. 138-140].

Looking at the old photographs of the rooms of the Batlló house [fig. 123-126, 129, 131-138, 140-142, 145] it is impossible not to be struck by their proximity to some of the descriptions of the quintessential *fin-de-siècle* home, the *demeure* understood as a place of inalienable property, mental space of the self and its true possessions, a nervous, radical interior [fig. 73-75], from Huysmans to the Goncourts, from Montesquiou to the Countess of Castiglione, from Pierre Loti to D'Annunzio ... Baudelaire spoke in 'La chambre double' of a room 'that resembles a dream, a truly *spiritual* room, where the stagnant atmosphere is lightly tinted pink and blue'.[48] In the Batlló house the popular images of the caves and grottoes of the universal exhibitions, those festivals of merchandise visited by millions of people, combine with the atmosphere of the spiritual house, whose aim is precisely to oppose that festival without qualities. But we have already noted that the condition of the

fig. 132

fig. 133

fig. 134

fig. 135

rhythm of fashion is to merge the most distinguished and select with the popular. What happens in the Batlló house is also what happens in the *maison d'artiste*, the refuge at the end of the world of the decadent. When Huysmans, in his novel *À rebours*, describes the dining room of Des Esseintes's house, whose windows have been replaced by portholes that do not open to the exterior but look into aquariums that the light passes through, can we avoid thinking of the *Nautilus*, Captain Nemo's submarine, the self-imposed prison of a free man, a prince who in revolt against the world has chosen to bury himself with all his treasures? These treasures—paintings, jewellery, books, extraordinary furniture—are suddenly lit up, at the very moment that we realize we are in a submarine, by the shifting greenish light of the seabed, which penetrates through large oblong hatches, actual windows separated by slender columns, as depicted by Neuville in the famous illustrations of the Hetzel octavo original edition [fig. 139].

The lobbies and rooms of the Batlló house—cave, seabed, aquarium—thus belong to that *fin-de-siècle* family, and to the radical—or neurotic or hysterical—interior of the *maison d'artiste*, that great simulacrum of the private. But then, unlike the great decadent models, the artist, in the Batlló house, was not the owner, selecting one by one, as true extensions of his *sickly* sensitivity, all of the objects; the house was made not by the person who would live in it—if anyone could truly be said to live in it—but by its architect.

In those same old photographs [fig. 133, 134], what do we find rubbing shoulders with the furniture designed by Gaudí? Vulgar carpets, common-or-garden lamps, mediocre chairs, dark paintings hung any old where, humdrum vases, all kinds of bibelots and even antiquated armchairs in the Spanish style, all mixed together and filling the whole space in a bric-à-brac typical of the bourgeois apartment — typical, some would say, the worst taste. The legendary tales of the constant clashes between Gaudí and Batlló throughout the course of the work are fully borne out by the photographs of those rooms, which give the impression of containing two utterly divergent interpretations of the space for living in: that of the artist, who designed the grottoes, sea beds and wooden furniture, and that of the owner, who has occupied the space with his things, as always, as he saw fit.

I referred above to a story published—in 1900, precisely—by Adolf Loos, one of the fiercest enemies of the artist-architect, about a 'poor little rich man'.[49] The protagonist has had a house built and decorated, down to the smallest details, by one of the most celebrated members of the Vienna Secession.

fig. 136, 137

Une fenêtre ouverte sur ces abîmes inexplorés. (Page 146.)

fig. 138, 139, 140

From that moment on, his house is complete—*full* and *harmonious*—and so is his life: he can no longer receive a gift or buy anything new, there will be nothing he can fall in love with. He is finished: he can no longer desire anything more. At the end of the story, Loos has him wandering like a ghost past the windows of the city's shops with their displays of goods that will never be for him.

The realization of the dream of overconsumption—the *maison d'artiste*—petrifies the market, turns it to stone. Baudelaire spoke of a room with a *stagnant* atmosphere. Isn't that impossible suspension, that isolation what the 1900s architect sought? The cave, the aquarium, the *house without windows* that, set apart from the anonymous flows of the city and exempt from the laws of equivalence of the market, exaggerates the virtues of its uniqueness. Such a house is evidently in conflict with the everyday, with *life*: it can never have *inhabitants*. But it is precisely this conflict, as we have been, that gives the Modernista architect his eccentric prestige and his popularity: his modern advantages [fig. 143-144].

Gaudí himself is the protagonist of a very local, Catalan version of the 'poor little rich man' story: the verse *auca* by Josep Carner I mentioned above,[50] in which a Mrs Comes, her house newly decorated, receives an unexpected gift of an Erard grand piano: a grand piano for which she can find no place in her living room, although it is far from clear if the problem is only its size. Indeed, a 'subtle' neighbour exclaims, on seeing it, 'The piano is the wrong style!'. The grand piano, therefore, neither fits in the room nor harmonizes with the décor, each failing the fault of the other: this house, too, is closed to objects from outside; it is finished, it is already harmonious and full. Carner's rhyming couplets start with a roll call of Gaudí's extraordinary works: the Sagrada Família, Park Güell, the Calvet house, the Batlló house where he 'provokes [or pokes] the foolish onlooker', and the Milà house, where 'he may be said to flatten him' ... Could this be more pointed? So great is Gaudí's prestige, however, that Mrs Comes turns to him to solve her problem. It now becomes clear that the question is more of style than of size: 'Without prejudice to art / where do we put this Erard?'. Gaudí's response, after measuring the room, looking under the carpets and moving the chairs around is: 'Take up the violin'. Faced with the genius of the artist the client must change her tastes: like the onlooker, she is a fool.

The circumstances on which these satirical verses were based have to do with Gaudí's decoration, between 1901 and 1904, of the apartment of the Marquis of Castelldosrius on the occasion of his marriage to Isabel Güell, who was a pianist, but the story has also been linked to the construction of the Batlló house: it is certainly not true, but it is significant. Because, in all honesty, to whom could Gaudí dedicate the construction of that underwater cave, that *belly*, but himself, as his identification of himself as the original creator, as demiurge?

Let us look for a moment at one of the smaller objects in the Batlló house: the oak chair Gaudí designed for the dining room [fig. 141, 142]. First, the wood from which it is made seems to have lost its compactness, its robustness, all the intrinsic properties of wood. The seat spills over at the sides and behind and the matter is concentrated at the edges, as it would be under the pressure of a seated person's weight if it were made of dough; the backrest, meanwhile, has sprouted flanges on which there is a circular recess as if someone had lifted the chair by its back and, in gripping it, their thumbs had met with so little resistance as to leave two round impressions in it; finally, the legs bend and twist round on themselves, as if in their softness they were buckling under the weight of the chair itself. Forms, then, that have been imposed on the material, with scant regard to its qualities, making it a mere passive recipient. Rather than the material expressing itself through its qualities, it is the form alone that speaks. In effect, what is this chair but the transcription in wood of moulded clay?

In saying this, however, we are accounting for only part of the meaning of this little work. In fact, this form is in its turn the consequence of an action or, more precisely here, of the pressure exercised by the weight of a body on it. Thus, even if we disregard the material that contains it, the form does not only express itself, as we suggested, but speaks of something else: a weight, a body, the pressure of a hand, of fingers still present in the impressions they have left. In other words, that chair, of an unexpectedly softened wood, is marked by the weight and the fingers —why not?—of Gaudí. The result could not be more disturbing: the Batllós' will have to sit on *his* chair, in his living mould; this is the meaning, though the legend has it that Gaudí used his workers to obtain these forms in the soft clay.

In leaving the marks of his body, thrusting his fingers into alienated, chaotic matter, what was Gaudí doing but recreating the act of the Creator, who not only gave form to the clay but, breathing on it, gave it life? Wasn't that the most traditional—and the most religious, the most *fin-de-siècle*—image of the inspired, possessed artist? The material disappears as such, buried in 'matter', surrendered to the force of the artist and *trans-formed* by it. Accordingly, and increasingly over the course of his career, Gaudí's forms are as immediate as a handprint: they come from a gesture that does not admit corrections or *pentimenti*, because it is directly and simultaneously the creative gesture and the gesture of the Creator.

fig. 141, 142

fig. 143, 144, 145

Undoubtedly, this vision of matter as something indifferent to the material, of matter *against* the material, is what most clearly separates the Gaudí of the Batlló house from his initial positions on the question of ornament, discussed in the previous chapter. In his works from here on, indeed, there will be no design but simply transmission: this is the origin of forms that go beyond the representation of the world or its imitation: forms, in short, given by the divinity. All of the legends of the inspired artist, of the artist as *alter deus,* have to do with what is expressed by Gaudí's handprint or his weight on the inert matter: that is the origin of his *enthusiasm,* of his *passion,* those virtues of the genius. And also, of course, of his particular *naturalism.*

But in the last analysis what was Gaudí doing but transcendently interpreting that *need* he continually referred to in his notes on ornamentation, so many years before? From the smallest—the chairs of soft paste, the larvae-like ceramics of the lobby, the eroded mouldings of the columns—to the largest—the staircases as giant fossil backbones, the rooms as caves, the vortex of the ceiling in the main living room [fig. 134]: everything is presented, essentially, as the original mass, the raw material into which the artist breathes form or, better yet, the principle of form to which amorphous matter necessarily tends, that matter desires. The celebration of nature is the celebration of the myths it contains, myths of the origin and of truth: the cave is the maternal womb of the earth; the sea is the medium in which everything emerges in the beginning. Gaudí's world, then, is not a house, the Batllós' house, but the *perpetuum mobile,* the eternal origin; the place where God and the artist swap powers, and also the place where creator and creation are confused. The interiors of the Batlló house are a mental aquarium in which the irrational, the magmatic, is celebrated just when the artist halts it with a gesture, an instant to create the form that the formless craves.

Here, however, the forms conceal more than they reveal. In reality, this exaltation of an extremely sophisticated primordial nature by way of a no less sophisticated recreation of it is one of the bases of decadent *fin-de-siècle* aestheticism, which is able to find the virtues of the world only in its simulacra. Baudelaire wrote in the dedication to *Les Paradis artificiels* that 'true reality is only in dreams' and Huysmans, whose Des Esseintes wished that '[instead] of artificial flowers imitating real flowers, natural flowers should mimic the artificial ones', claimed that the mark of true genius was to be capable of 'substituting the dream of reality for the reality itself'.[51] But surely the same substitution was offered to the crowds at World's Fairs and even in the brightly lit windows of city shops?

fig. 146, following page fig. 147

Casa de
D. José Batlló Casanovas

A. Gaudí, Arquitecto
J. Badía Miarnau, Constructor

MATÉRIAUX ET DOCUMENTS D'ART ESPAGNOL

PLANCHE No 7

FAÇADE ✣ FAÇADE ✣ FACHADA ✣ FASSADE

PHOT. BRESSANINI

PHOTOTYPIE FARERA

BARCELONE

MAISON BATLLÓ — AVENUE DE GRACIA, 43

ARCHITECTE: A. GAUDI

BARCELONA

CASA BATLLÓ — PASEO DE GRACIA, 43

ARQUITECTO: A. GAUDI

fig. 148, 149, 150

If the artist aspires to standing at the apex of that great simulacrum, how far can this dream, this confusion between the generating force of nature, eternally yearning matter, and the *representation* of that force that is his creation, his work, be carried? In Gaudí's case, very far.

To begin with, let's look again at a relatively small element: the front doors of the apartments, made of oak, like the chairs we commented on before, and similarly softened. Standing out from their mass, clear and sharp, are stars, which send us off once again to the farthest points that the movement of cosmic creation can reach. Also protruding through the surface of the same mass, but barely suggested, are elongated forms with rounded ends, whose sinister insinuation is hard to escape: bones, tibias. In the magma awaiting that form the creator will give it we see the instant of the greatest and most brilliant concentration of matter, and at the same time catch a hint of what lies in the background: the skeleton. And is this not the theme of the most public and representative part of the house, the glazed gallery [fig. 147, 148]?

I have spoken elsewhere of the process of liquefaction that stone suffers here: waves, wrinkles, creases, holes with rounded edges, greats drops hanging in suspension ... The stone has lost its tectonic qualities and seems incapable not only of constructing the building, of erecting it, but even of supporting its own weight. Turned to lava, follows the downward course imposed by gravity and flows as if on this occasion the architect's hands, or his breath, had been unable to overcome that force. Only the hardest elements survive this process of softening of the stone, the decomposition of the compact body of matter: the columns, the tall tibias that give the Batlló house its popular name, 'the house of bones' [fig. 148-150]; and I am not surprised at their family resemblance to the 'Modernista cemetery' that Corominas, one of the *Cu-Cut!* illustrators most concerned with fashion, had drawn [fig. 151] ... in 1902! Bones all but stripped clean, to which still cling—as if to make all the more visible the process of putrefaction that has exposed them—a few shreds of that body's flesh.[52]

But the path that has brought us to this vision of *putrefactio* can also lead us in the other direction: the traces of flesh are perhaps, on the contrary, a new flowering and the bones, tibias, appear in openings whose form is quite evidently vulvar, genital. Behind them, in the main living room of the Batlló house is the generating maternal womb, the whirlwind of creation that, from the ceiling, is reflected everywhere. But, after all, it was precisely in the uterus that doctors of the time, starting with Charcot, one of Freud's first teachers, located the principle of hysteria. So what was fig. 151

y ben morts als que no deixondirán ni las trompetas del Judici perque de judici may n'han tingut ni'n tindrán. Comprenem en aquets tres grupos, respectivament, als morts aprofitats que han anat al Municipi a ferse els seus, als morts hipócritas que's fan l'abnegat y el redemptor y cobran a tant per discurs, y als morts mortals de necessitat que tenen las sevas sepulturas a la plassa Real y al carrer Nou de la Rambla. Precisament aquets morts son els qui esperavan la mort del catalanisme, peró com que es una veritat com una casa alló de "qui la mort d'un altre espera la seva veu primera", ara resulta que aquell a qui volían matar es qui'ls ha enterrat.

Altres morts més atrevits fins s'han arriscat a dir que l'havían mort al catalanisme a cops de sabre y de garrots de banya, peró a n'aquets tals se'ls hi pot dir alló de la comedia:

"Los muertos que vos matais
gozan de buena salud."

Prou n'han fet de cosas per matarnos, peró com que som *cuatro gatos*, a set vidas per barba representém la friolera de vintivuit vidas, lo que equival a dir que se 'ls gira feyna y que no's pot matar tot lo que es gras y que per més que's fassi sempre resultará que entre morts y ferits... una sabata plena.

Y permétinme que aquí posi l'obligat R. I. P. perque no més que de registrar tanta mortandat, e's asseguro que estich més mort que viu.

LLEIXIU.

TEMPS A VENIR

Si prospera el modernisme com ara va prosperant, prou veurém els cementiris totalment modernisats.

TOT ES SEGÓNS EL COLOR...

—Manel, qué tens?
—Estich trist.
—Estás trist?
—Y molt!
—¿Qué't passa?
T'has disgustat ab algú?
Cóntam. Ja sabs que m'agrada
serví ab tot als meus amichs
y tú ets un d'ells.
—Moltas gracias
—Si et fa falta algún quartet
per acabar la mesada,
ja pots contar que es tot teu
lo que porto a la butxaca.
—No'm fa falta cap diner.
—Donchs parla que estich ab ansia.
—No'm passa res, prô estich trist.
—Això ho contas a n'en Sarrias.
No t'ocurreix res de nou,
no t'ha passat cap desgracia,
tens diners, segóns tú dius,
y em vens ab aquesta cara?
—¿Que potser tinch mal color?
—Un color d'aquells que espanta.
—¿Color de fel sobreixit?
—¡Cál pitjor. De prunas agras,
per l'istil dels que en Nonell
gasta per pintar gitanas.
No siguis tonto, Manel,
y explicat d'una vegada.
—Donsas mira; t'ho diré
tan sols en una paraula...
¿No sabs a quin dia estém?
—Tinch el calendari a casa,
prô fa temps que no he cobrat
y es un dato que no falla,
ara de segur que som
del trenta nou al quaranta.

Gaudí doing here? From what level of consciousness—since we have mentioned Freud—have these forms emerged? I would like to recall in passing a couple of examples. On the one hand, a passage in *L'uomo di genio,* (The Man of Genius)[53] the popular book by the criminal anthropologist Cesare Lombroso,[54] first published in 1888: in the 'Obscenity' section, among other instances of works produced by 'erotomaniacs, paralytics and demented patients' whose principal characteristic is 'the most shameless obscenity' Lombroso recounts how 'a cabinet-maker would carve virile members at every corner of a piece of furniture, or at the summits of trees. This, too, recalls many works of savages and of ancient races, in which the organs of sex are everywhere prominent'. On the other hand, a couple of drawings that Picasso made in Barcelona around 1902 or 1903, which are very close to Gaudí, then, both spatially and chronologically [fig. 152, 153]. In one, a couple making love are attentively observed by a cat, a distant memory of *Olympia,* or of *Olympia* 'before' being painted by Manet: on the headboard we see finials carved in the form of penises, long form undulating mouldings and symmetrical vaginal forms. In the other drawing a woman lying on her front gazes at us from a bed whose carved uprights, topped by small glandes, are reminiscent of the famous bones of the Batlló gallery, while on the wall behind here we see again, but now much larger, a stylized vagina. In these Picasso drawings, then, the obsessions of that Lombrosian cabinetmaker, parodic culmination of the decadent object whose form derives from the *nervous life* and prolongs the mood of its owner, seem to have been made tangible in a Gaudí-esque ornamentation. That that ornamentation caused Gaudí to be reviled equally by the champions of good taste, the *esprit contemporain,* and by the advocates of de-ornamentation—in the interpretative line of criminal anthropology, what better proof that ornamentation is a crime than these Gaudí-esque ornamental *obscenities*?—or that years later it was to be the object of the pathographic studies of Bückmann,[55] where that now distant equation of 'genius and madness' as proposed by Lombroso in criminal terms should have continued to resonate is not what concerns us now. What is of interest here, when we contemplate those carvings that Picasso drew on the headboards of the two beds, is how a popular mass-market ornamental system, luxuriant in the most literal sense of the word, could find a place in the work of Gaudí, overflowing it: I spoke of the whirlwind of creation, which behind the vaginal openings is present everywhere, from the vortex of the living-room ceiling to the little differently-shaped swirls carved on the oak doors, or the dozens of these that would have covered the floor if Gaudí managed to pave it with the hexagonal tiles he had designed for this project but was only able to use later, in the Milà house: spirals in which, as we well know, sea creatures—octopus and starfish—revolve.

fig. 152, 153

From the abysmal depths to the heavens, matter—*mater, matrix*—revolves, continuously creating itself. There is nothing strange, then, in the presence here of putrefaction, whose traditional symbolism, always expressed in funeral forms such as bones, always alludes to both the end of life and to rebirth. Or, more precisely, to the ability of matter to regenerate itself.

The Batlló house is on the one hand a huge *vanitas* exhibited on Barcelona's most elegant boulevard, and as a *vanitas* is a reminder, unexpectedly emerging from the luxury of the bourgeois townhouse, of the transience of all things and of their destiny, death; on the other, holding open the doors of the womb of nature, it is the image of germination, the endlessly repeated principle of all things. The power of nature, represented by its eternal metamorphosis, *seems* to be the *theme* of the Batlló house; time devours matter and matter, continually reverting to chaos, constantly seeks form, in the whirlwind of its *perpetuum mobile*. Gaudí, Francesc Pujols wrote, 'fleeing from compromises arrives at prehistory'.[56] Or beyond: can there be any better justification for the stubborn existence of the artist?

The photographer Pere Vivas has drawn my attention to a detail of the Batlló house as seemingly insignificant as it is extraordinary. It too is on the oak doors of the apartments. These apartments are identified not in the normal way, with numbers—of the floor and of the door—but with letters, and, again contrary to normal practice, not with the same letters, *A* and *B*, on each floor, but, in ascending order, from *A* on the first floor to *I* on the top. On each landing, the ends of the wrought-iron railing form a circle with a trefoil or triquetra inside it [fig. 155], except for one, which contains a spiral: that circle corresponds to the door of apartment *G* [fig. 154, 156]. This *G* is in the form of a spiral and the spiral is an ancient symbol associated with the growth of the universe, with its evolution: the form of the nebula, the cosmos in motion. It is also the initial letter of 'generation' and 'genesis'. And of Gaudí, of course: in the artist's initial is the vortex of all that is engendered.

Confusing Creation and Creator, and confusing the Creator and the architect—that is to say, sliding into pantheistic heterodoxy and falling into the sin of pride—Gaudí, so strict a believer, takes to their extreme the typical temptations of the *fin-de-siècle* artist: the vortex of the whirlwind is the apex of the market.

The artist has the power to suspend form, but turned into a metaphor for its changes it becomes petrified, turning the artist, as I said, into a new and terrible Midas: the gingerbread house will in the end be exchanged for a treasure of hard

fig. 154

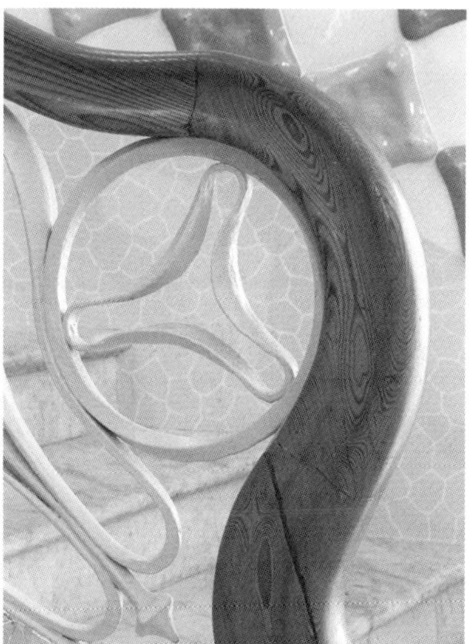

fig. 155, 156

L'ARQUITECTE
I EL DIABLE

diamonds that no one can eat. Dissolving the soul in the simulacrum of nature is not the same as selling it, but beyond certain limits—and this the decadents, always so ready to be hypnotized by the beauty of hell, knew very well—it is hard to tell whether the inspiration comes from God or the devil.

L'arquitecte i el diable (The architect and the devil) is the title of a trite moralistic tale by Jordi Català (Jaume Bonfill) published in the Patufet collection of children's books[57]. On the cover, a drawing by Lluís Mallol shows the devil offering a roll of plans to a young man and pointing upwards with his finger to indicate the glory that can be his—in exchange for his soul, of course [fig. 157]. At the root of all this, inevitably, is a competition: the king of the country wishes to build a palace that, once again, will be eccentric and ever new, that will 'set itself apart from known constructions and never grow old'. Naturally, our architect, in the grip of his desire to create, turns his back on the world: 'irascible and dry', for him there is nothing but 'what constitutes his obsession', his work, although having sold his soul and won the competition his popularity will be such that he can think of nothing but 'his own pleasure' (in Catalan, *en el propi gaudi*). There follows, of course, repentance, tears of contrition, forgiveness, the anchorite retreat: in short, true glory.

It is highly significant that in the Barcelona of the early decades of the twentieth century Faust should be represented by an architect, and one who's life, moreover, coincides perfectly with the myth of Gaudí, whose conflicts with clients multiplied from the Batlló house on: dismissed from the restoration of Palma Cathedral in Mallorca, accused by the cathedral chapter of slighting the opinions of others — of pride, precisely; dismissed from the Milà house by a client who refused to accept the imposition of his symbols and sued him for what was an astronomical sum at that time, he was the most *expensive* artist, now unmatchable, who at a certain point in time turned his back on the world—after being a dandy in his youth, as his legend persists in explaining—and, shut up in his studio, surrounded by hundreds of plaster casts [fig. 150, 158], by an overflow of desiring matter, under the shadow of the Sagrada Família—the new cathedral, the last great temple—will now work only for the superior client that the angry architect, the chosen one, deserves: God's architect, he was called, in the end, by his contemporaries.

fig. 157

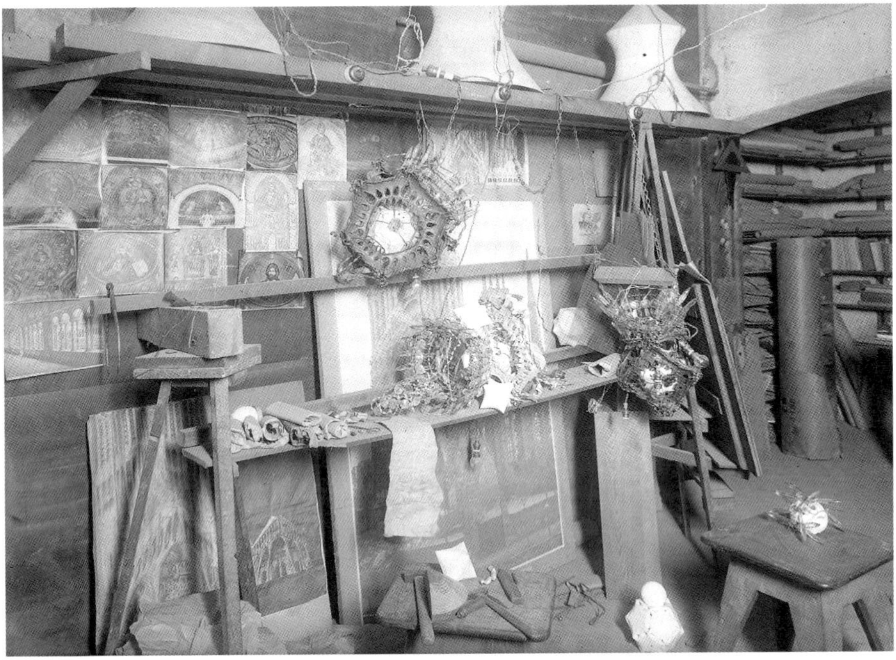

fig. 158

472

FIRE AND ASHES

Behold the Work of Restoration of Capitalism

As we recalled in the previous chapter, in 1912, in *Picarol,* commenting on a cartoon by Josep Aragay depicting a line of quivering buildings [fig. 96], their jumbled profiles like bundled skeins ending in towers that seem to dissolve into a night sky dotted with stars that are sparks flying up from the dissolution of those same buildings, under which a multitude streams *en masse,* or literally as mass, like lava at the foot of their eruption (but perhaps everything is more ingenuous than I am suggesting), Francesc Pujols [58] compared the fires of the Tragic Week[59] with works built by 'the architects of the city of Barcelona' who were, he claimed, three in number: 1st, Mr Gaudí; 2nd, Mr Domènech i Montaner, and 3rd, Mr Puig i Cadafalch. Both groups, the arsonists and the architects, had turned Barcelona into a city 'in flames'; both were 'out-and-out revolutionaries', with the difference that one made their revolution 'from below, from the street' and the other 'from the top of the buildings they erect'; those 'true architects of Barcelona's *continual* revolution,' Pujols went on, 'perpetuate in bricks and stone the soul that sustains us, and have the courage to start over again, as if nothing had happened'.

In a city in which, almost three years later, the effects of the Tragic Week could still be seen on all sides, whose empty lots and buildings in ruins were constant reminders of the fires and the destruction, and which was unable to forget the fierce repression and summary executions because it was still living in the aftermath of that repression; a city in which fear was embedded along with the belief that beneath appearances, always latent, in an ill-defined subsoil, there lurked a heartless headless mob capable of suddenly bursting out with a pitiless and incomprehensible hatred (this was affirmed by bio-evolutionism, by criminal anthropology and by the special police units); a city in which arbitrary repression and firing squads had been used to reinstate, in the face of the formless terror—sinister in the precise sense of the term—of the masses, the concrete terror of the State—succinct deaths to petrify the fear—and establish this as a recognizable story amid the gigantic and shifting landscape of the columns of smoke, in order to assert the familiar against the strange, the regular against the mercenary, the name against anonymity, the face against the headless, the firing squad against the condemned, Good against Evil and, ultimately, Architecture against Rubble; in such a city, in short, the argument—or, rather, the image—that Pujols puts forward seems completely out of place: architects as arsonists, what is on top like what is below, construction as destruction, continual revolution and starting over again ... But that image of burning buildings, of the city that consumes itself in its own fires and also constructs itself in them, is the metaphor of the modern city, the merchandise-city that ceaselessly devours and vomits itself. Pujols's Barcelona is not, then, that city of neoclassical form and precise functioning, celebratory and productive in harmoniously balanced parts, proposed by the intellectuals and technocrats of *Noucentisme*[60] and invested with thaumaturgic powers in the dreams of a bourgeoisie that was also in equal parts enlightened and fearful, but a savage city, abandoned to genius and to rage, to furious individualism and to the formless crowd, whose light comes on the one hand, and at one extreme, from burning churches and convents and on the other from the most deliriously eccentric buildings, and whose generation is produced, whether through fire or through *new* construction, in its destruction. As if there were no distances or intermediate spaces in the city, as if it did not exist except in the tension between that which is razed to its foundations and that which is raised up without foundations, that which is without precedent: the new, the great idol that replaces the little idols burned in the churches. If Pujols's city has, in other words, a recognized value, it is that of change/exchange, which renders all things equivalent: what goes down comes up; what is burned to the ground twinkles in the sky with the same fires; what is destroyed, is constructed; hatred is brilliant and genius is rabid. Exchange value, in effect: are not these the figures of the perfect *laissez-faire*? Pujols says just that: they are all revolutionaries, and what he does, in essence, is simply describe the capitalist city, and quite crudely. At the end of the day, the comparison between those old churches and monasteries reduced to vacant lots by the revolutionary masses and the buildings constructed by the modern architects—also revolutionary, also incandescent—that rise up absolutely new is none other than the extreme plastic image of a kind of urgent, violent and necessarily comprehensive ecclesiastical confiscation or secularization, and also of its revenues, its profits. The destructive violence generated by the class struggle clears the site, leaving it free for the market, and the modern architects give to the fruits of speculation the most appropriate forms: in other words, the most fervidly individualistic, the most *outré* forms. In its destruction and its construction, in consuming and producing itself as a commodity, the city has been transformed into the constant spectacle of itself.

Perhaps one of the photographs that appeared so often at that time, in newspapers and on postcards, showing the panorama from Montjuïc of Barcelona with its burning churches, the columns of smoke rising vertically against the backdrop of the mass of streets and houses, would be the perfect image, both literal and metaphorical, of the city on fire proclaimed by Pujols [fig. 159]. Accounts of the Tragic Week tell of people all over Barcelona gathered on roof terraces to gaze on the spectacle that these photographs replicate with the mechanicity of the camera and freeze forever. These images ensure the permanence of the smoke, fixing it as a sign of that which no longer exists. Down through the years it has been possible to point a finger at the plumes of smoke in the photographs, as people did in those July days on the housetops, and identify the church or monastery from which they rise, which has already disappeared. All the power of the bird's-eye view is projected onto a city transformed into a great hypostyle hall whose columns, rising from the subsoil, give an idea of the gigantic buildings that will be constructed there: always changing but always the same, like the loops of smoke, and as mesmerizing. The burning city is mesmerizing, and the panoramas shown in those pictures, each one an authentic *Spectacula Babylonica*, are the most radically perfect image of the urbanism of the contemporary Barcelona. All that is needed, as Pujols says, is for the 'soul that sustains us'—that is to say, the smoke—to be perpetuated in bricks and stone; in bricks and stone that will also be like smoke, and that was the task of the most eccentric architects, with Gaudí first among them.

In fact, years later, in 1927, Pujols was to give a new version, an extreme version of the same aesthetic figurations of the merchandise-city. In *La visió artística i religiosa d'en Gaudí* (The Artistic and Religious Vision of Gaudí) he wrote with regard to the Sagrada Família that Catalonia was 'destined to sacrifice the Catholic religion, dedicating cathedrals to it, the most fundamentally artistic cathedral in the world'. This is the metaphor that Pujols now uses to explain such a sacrifice: '...it is the case with those that, raising pigs for slaughter, give them all they can to fatten them so that weigh what they ought to when the day comes to sacrifice them [...] and everyone knows that no part of the pig goes to waste.'[61]

following page fig. 159

UNA FOTOGRA

Vista parcial de Barcelona, desde la monta

Montjuich, el miércoles de la semana trágica

Los Sucesos de Barcelona del día 27 de Julio de 1909

fig. 160, 161

Catalonia, Pujols says in this hair-raising way, fattens up Catholicism by feeding it the 'confused, Baroque and monstrous' style of Gaudí's gigantic temple,[62] and then devours it in its entirety and feeds off it. The most characteristic obsessions of Spanish anticlericalism, and, of course, the unavoidable rituals of the church burners and murderers and devourers of priests and nuns seem suddenly to shrink in Pujols's brutal depictions: Baroque monstrosity of images, which reaches its highest point in the ecstatic vision of the flames that will reduce them to ashes, sacrifice and cannibalism.

But it is not surprising that for Pujols the Sagrada Família should incarnate —I believe that is the right word—these things, or the *process* of these things: the endless exploitation of the city as an enormous pigsty. Rising slowly but without pause in the midst of a half empty Eixample, overflowing with images that seem to gush forth from its not yet solidified stone, the stump of a temple without limits, it can be the metaphor at once of the gate to a new city, of the volcanic eruption of its energy and of the flames that consume it, and also of the contrary: if this is a gate it leads nowhere, if it is an eruption it is an eruption of its most archaic forms, and if it is fire, its flames are already petrified. And back to the beginning again. Temple as ruin, ruin as mountain, mountain as temple: Joan Maragall[63] had already used these metaphors, and especially that of 'destruction as construction', in which the most transcendent grandeur and the most complete uselessness are mixed in the same circle.[64] 'Confused, Baroque and monstrous': the Sagrada Família is the place from which the images of the great contradiction can break off and where they can be fixed, par excellence [fig. 160, 161, 196].

But since we have mentioned him, let's talk about Maragall. As a good bourgeois, at the outbreak of the Tragic Week, on July 26, 1909, he was on holiday outside Barcelona, in Caldetes.[65] There, with his family, as he wrote, 'the sad days passed in material peace'.[66] In September, when the ashes no less than revenge began to be cooled by the ice and iron of immoderate repression, Maragall began to write the articles that all through the summer the living forces of the city had been calling out for. The first two, 'Ah! Barcelona ...' and 'The Burned Church', were published in *La Veu de Catalunya*, in October and December 1909 respectively; the third, written between the other two, in the days when the death sentences that resulted in the firing squads on Montjuïc were issued, 'The City Of Forgiveness', was banned and never published.[67]

Schematizing a good deal, but schematizing according to the same script that Maragall put forward in those articles, what was so shocking as to require censorship—and to censor Maragall, hailed as the poet-prophet of an entire people, was a matter of no little importance—was the way the author openly challenged the official explanation of the 'events': an official version that ignored the real causes—beginning with the most immediate: opposition to conscription for the war in Morocco—and essentially attributed the unrest to foreigners, to outsiders, to a kind of ubiquitous mercenary mob, and presented the burning of churches and religious buildings as a confrontation between Good and Evil, God and the devil. In his first article, in which he specifically referred to the Pastoral that Torras i Bages,[68] bishop of Vic, had published on the fire-raising, Maragall denied that it was simply a case of 'Satan against God, the Principle of Evil against the Redemption, Hatred against Love' and rejected, more subtly but no less emphatically, the idea that 'the remedy to this, simple and sublime' was 'to embrace the Cross, to suffer martyrdom as a glory'; also, and more importantly, he spoke out against the elusive interpretations of politicians and the Catalan nationalist press, from Prat de la Riba[69] to Eugeni d'Ors,[70] denying that 'the ones that do the evil are outsiders': 'Do not attempt to tell me it was those people,' he wrote, and flatly declared, 'it is us', before adding, with not a hint of irony, that the 'excellence' of the Barcelonese consisted in 'the bomb and blasphemy' and that Barcelona had to 'accept the bombs'. Finally, as the title of the censored article, 'The City Of Forgiveness', eloquently stated, in place of the tremendous repression and the executions that followed the revolt he proposed reconciliation.

But let's leave this issue, already amply explored, here.[71] I want to focus now on how Maragall concludes that sentence about the excellence of the bombs and blasphemy to which I referred above: 'tell me if you do not see in this as a ray of light ... dark light'. Typical of Maragall's taste for contradiction and his oracular tone, an echo of the 'beam of darkness' of the mystics and of a fearful interpretation—fearful of God and of his death, or his fate—of Nietzsche's aurora, the phrase is magnificent. Elsewhere, for example in his articles on the Sagrada Família, Gaudí's temple, Maragall had referred, as I have just mentioned, to the emotion aroused in him on seeing destruction as construction, and that phrase encapsulates this idea: it is, literally the myth of the 'clean slate', which in Maragall takes the form of an iconomachy typical of the imperfect nihilism of 'his' modernity. As such, the bombs and the fires are in the very being of the Barcelonese, he says, and are their way of cleansing, of clearing, of making room. When Maragall writes 'Barcelona, you have to suffer if you want to save yourself ... you have to accept the bombs', what should we think we are reading if not some kind of radical proposal for renewal? Against the immobility—in the literal sense of the word—of the official interpretation, Maragall proposes the 'dynamism' of a society that will 'necessarily' have to modernize, and proposes it through the destruction and demolition, or at least, if not quite that, through its metaphors: the bombs and blazing torches of the revolutionaries would have in some way been the instrument, as unexpected as it was unconscious, with which society had provided itself for this renewal. Could there be a more forthright image of the capitalist condition of the city, the *laissez-faire* on which the city has continually to transform itself? And above all, could there be a clearer statement of what the revolutionary destruction was for? To contribute to the revolution, of course, but not exactly to the one that the destroyers 'from below, from the street', as Pujols wrote, imagined. To paraphrase Ernst Friedrich, here too we could say that the destruction of the Tragic Week was 'the work of restoration of capitalism'.[72]

The theory that those fires, like other modes of iconoclastic destruction in other places and other times, exercised the function of an immediate and radical secularization—we shall talk about this in a moment—seems perfectly fulfilled in that 'ray of light ... dark light' cast, according to Maragall, by the bombs of the revolutionaries. But we should temper the enthusiasm of our interpretations. Certainly, many of the plots that resulted from these destructions were 'sold off', 'secularized', and in most cases it was the Church itself—as so often—that speculated with them, but the truth is that at no time were there major urban operations, and in fact many of the buildings ravaged by fire were rebuilt and resumed their former functions, as many of them continue to do today.[73] The form of secularization admirably exposed in Maragall's text, with its shades and nuances and, above all, with its great force of metaphor, represents the most clearly 'economic' side of the fires of that week in July. But that is little, very little, and too imperfect. There must be more, and, of course, that beam of dark light leads us into other realms and to another 'economy' that I will not say is not an 'artistic economy.' But to engage with this question we shall have to talk about the third article: 'The Burned Church'.

Maragall writes here of the impression made on him by the first Mass in one of the burned churches: 'I have never attended a Mass like that. The vault of the church fallen in, the walls blackened and flaking, the altars destroyed, missing, especially the great black void at the end, where the main altar had been ... a torrent of sunlight streamed through the crack in the vault with swarms of flies hovering in the glare ....' But for Maragall this was, as we can imagine, not a desolate prospect of destruction, but the sublime vision of restoration: 'destroying the church you have restored the Church ... the fire has built, the blasphemy has cleansed.' From the dust, the debris, the flies, the wind and the sunlight penetrating the church, Maragall sees 'a new and current virtue' emerge.

Obviously, Maragall is speaking here—as I said before—in oracular terms: he is the augur. However, behind that restoration of a purer church—'the hatred of Christ has reinstated Christ in his house'—a church closer to its origins, purged of pomp and ceremony, given back to 'the early Christians' and once again capable of relating iconoclasm with attempts at reform—and it is precisely the Reformation that resonates here—there is something else, something very *fin-de-siècle*, something very typical of an 'economy' of symbolism and *décadentisme*, something, in short, very subtly and profoundly—structurally—reordering.

Let's look at the qualities of that virtue: 'new and current'. For virtue to be new is what the Reformation had always sought: there, without paradox, lies its fixed eternity; but if this 'new' virtue is compromised, not to say undermined, by its 'current' condition, in which it is nothing more than a momentary circumstance, the aesthetic vision is the solution to this contradiction. In that temple in ruins (and what an extensive tragicomic iconography attaches to it, starting with Burke's famous essay on the sublime!)[74] shot through by a beam of light in which the grains of dust brilliantly vibrate and the flies dance—that is to say, in the corpuscular atmosphere of the ruin of the temple—we see not its virtue but, obviously, the *image* of its virtue. Maragall is transported and transports us, then, not to a discourse but to a vision. The images, the volutes and the tinsel of the churches have literally vanished thanks to the revolutionary fires, in such a way that, unconsciously, society has given back to itself—great catharsis—the truth of the bare walls.

What we have here, for a start, is the first principle of the invention of 'Catalan Gothic', bare and austere, horizontal and 'democratic', about which our historians have had so much to say, as if the Baroque were not with us and its successive destructions would have been a blessing—a silent and hidden artistic blessing: blessed iconoclasm, then. But I am not going to talk about that now. Nor about what I have already insinuated: the *décadentiste* background of that aesthetic vision of ruin as construction, seen in nothing more and nothing less than a church, in the middle of the Mass ... although it would do no harm here to turn briefly to the ineffable Barbey d'Aurevilly or Huysmans and the similar way in which they both narrate their conversion to Catholicism through the experience—from the aesthetic sentiment of the sublime—of a solemn Mass. Certainly, they worship a church that, to paraphrase

Baudelaire, 'glorifies the cult of images', but when all is said and done they also fail to distinguish clearly between the smoke of the incense or of the incendiary, and between the gleam of gold and that of fire. Consider, for example, the things that can happen in books ranging from Barbey d'Aurevilly's *L'Ensorcelée* to Huysmans's *La Cathédrale*.[75] Didn't Max Nordau, in his hugely popular *Entartung*—with which we dealt at some length in *On Loos, Ornament and Crime: Columns of Smoke Vol. II*[76]—write, precisely in relation to the decadent dandy, of the 'abysmally dark symbolism' of the Catholicism of these personages?[77] Maragall knew them well, those same fumes, emerging as he did from the same kind of humus, although they were full of irony and he was not: one pomp for another, and an end to it. What I want to do is simply to point out that the 'new and current' quality of this 'aesthetic economy'—or, to put it another way, of that ideology: structure and superstructure meet in this 'economy'—was reflected in the hundreds of photographs that were published in the days and weeks following the rebellion [fig. 162-192]. The Barcelona revolutionaries of 1909 burned schools, nursing homes, convents, churches, paintings, sculptures and all kinds of furniture, furnishings and religious objects. Like all iconoclasts they were convinced, and rightly so, of the identity between the power of the represented and the power of its representation: those buildings and those images were not the expression of a power, but were possessed of it, *they had power*. Now, what was to emerge from the clean slate of destruction was not only, as Pujols noted, new revenues for the merchandise-city, its *fireworks*, but also new images, which are the images of its destruction, its photographs. Of the various series of postcards that were produced of the Tragic Week, the most impressive is undoubtedly the collection of one hundred views published by A.T.V. (the initials of Àngel Toldrà Viazo), carefully numbered 1 to 100 and titled *Events of Barcelona* [fig. 162-183]. Children on a mound of rubble, a woman hurrying past with her laundry basket [fig. 180], a man leaning on his cane contemplating the remains of a façade [fig. 178], teams of rubble clearers pausing to smoke a cigarette [fig. 169], policemen with rifles standing guard at the doors of ruined buildings [fig. 162, 181] ... But even so, despite these people, the photographs show an empty city. The important thing is the buildings: desolate interiors in which the vaults and the floors have collapsed and from which the furniture, be it sacred or functional, has completely disappeared, its only remnants the fading charcoal ghosts on the walls where the images had stood on their pedestals [fig. 174]—exceptionally, a spectacularly twisted bed base bares its iron springs in the foreground [fig. 183], in the most absolute solitude—and exteriors in which the smoke is still present in soot-smudged door and window frames [fig. 162, 166, 168, 169, 180], almost always photographed from the top of a neighbouring building to show the fallen-in roofs and the landscape of the rest of the city stretching to the horizon [fig. 172] of the most distant houses—and to show, too, the factory chimneys, smoking in their turn, smoking again, smoke signals of the darkest starting over again[fig. 175]. The power of these *realist* photographic images replaces the power of those others, those old idols of wood, plaster and embroidered fabric that have disappeared, so that what we see of them is precisely their disappearance.

But these images also systematically hold up before our eyes, time and again, that same vision of which Maragall spoke. The photographers of the A.T.V. postcards took good care to ensure that the destroyed churches should indeed be seen as ruins, and not as piles of rubble or demolition sites, and, even more, as sublime ruins: in the naves of the denuded churches, beams of sunlight almost always slant down through densely corpuscular air, atmospheres of revelation—all of them converted by fire and photography, by each and by both, into Byzantine churches—to fall on the vacant places of the missing main altars, and set them on fire again, but this time through the presence of their—rather than His—heat: in other words, what shines there in that beams of light is not the power of the divine but—so very differently—that of photography, here more than ever *photo-graphy* [fig. 165, 173, 174, 176, 177].

In these photos, the marks of the fire are the signs of the necessary wounds of restoration, and are presented as such: repeated, serial, standardized, reproduced thousand times, printed, marketed, sold, mailed ... At the same time as the images of the saints and the gilded volutes of the altars and altarpieces were disappearing in the smoke of fires, the photographic images, more powerful than any others, of a 'new and current' time were appearing on those postcards.

To understand in plastic terms that power of photography, at once substitutive and affirmative, we need only make a comparison. As I have said, a lot of books appeared in the aftermath of the Tragic Week, almost all of them illustrated with photographs, brought out by popular publishers whose catalogues take full advantage of the most sensational issues of the day: crime, prostitution, slums and so on. What I would like to do now is to look more closely at the covers of some of the books published in the immediate wake of the facts, in 1909 or early 1910. For instance, the design of *The Tragic Week. Account of the Sedition and Fires in Barcelona and Catalonia*[78] adopts, perhaps unconsciously, the profile of an arched window: in the upper part we see 'seditious' workers shooting from behind a barricade at the agents of law and order deployed in perfect formation on the other side; in the larger lower part, personages whose faces naively correspond to the

A. T. V. — Sucesos de BARCELONA (26-31 de Julio de 1909)
14. Iglesia Parroquial de S. Juan. Gracia. Fachada lateral

A. T. V. — Sucesos de BARCELONA
(26-31 de Julio de 1909)
23 Iglesia de los Agonizantes. Interior
(Calle Baja de S. Pedro)

Sucesos de BARCELONA (26-31 de Julio de 1909)
8. Convento de Loreto. Uno de los dormitorios
despues del incendio

A. T. V. — Sucesos de BARCELONA (26-31 de Julio de 1909)
13. Interior de la Iglesia de San Andrés

fig. 162, 163, 164, 165

fig. 166, 167, 168

A. T. V. — Sucesos de BARCELONA. (26-31 de Julio de 1909)
30. Convento de PP. Franciscanos
Calle de Santaló. S. Gervasio

fig. 169, 170, 171

A. T. V. — Sucesos de BAR…LONA (26-31 de Julio de 190…
22. Ruinas de la …lesia de la Ayuda
(Calle Baja de S. Pedro)

A. T. V. — Sucesos de BARCELONA (26-31 de Julio de 1909)
32. Iglesia de los PP. de S. Felipe Neri. (Gracia)

fig. 172, 173, 174

A. T. V. — Sucesos de BARCELONA. (26-31 de Julio de 1909)
6. Convento de las Jerónimas. Vistas de las ruinas

A. T. V. — Sucesos de BARCELONA. (26-31 de Julio de 1909)
4. Interior de la Iglesia de S. Antonio Abad

A. T. V. — Sucesos de BARCELONA. (26-31 de Julio de 1909)
33. Interior de la Parroquia de S. Juan. Gracia

fig. 175, 176, 177

A. T. V. — Sucesos de BARCELONA. (26-31 de Julio 1909)
35. Misioneros del Sagrado Corazón de Maria.Gracia
Casa Misión y restos del Colegio

A. T. V. — Sucesos de BARCELONA. (26-31 de Julio de 1909)
72. Convento de P. P. Salesianos
Calle de Floridablanca

fig. 178, 179, 180

A. T. V. — Sucesos de BARCELONA (26-31 de Julio de 1909)
90. Puerta de la Iglesia de Santa Madrona (Nueva)

fig. 181, 182, 183

fig. 184, 185, 186

most clichéed stereotypes of hatred and rage found in treatises on the passions and to the classifications of male and female delinquents of the scientific police brandishing blazing torches, have violated the peace of a cloister and lunge towards a young girl protected by a nun whose solemnly upraised arm seems (not) to have the power to halt them [fig. 184]. There is also the anonymous *The Bloody Week (Barcelona Events)*:[79] a photomontage shows us, above, the cloister of a burned-out convent and, below, partially superposed or overlapping the ruin, the cut-out figure of a vigilant policeman armed with a rifle [fig. 185]. Last but not least we have *The Revolution of July in Barcelona. Its Repression. Its Victims. The Ferrer Trial*:[80] in the lower part the 'seditious' revolutionaries, in retreat, and with one of their number on the ground, fire from a distance at a barricade behind which we see the silhouettes of well-trained soldiers, while, above, absolute order reigns in the courtroom at the trial of Ferrer i Guardia,[81] in profile opposite the row of judges on the bench, between the silhouettes of a soldier with rifle and bayonet and a policeman [fig. 186].

These examples suffice to show how all of the book covers follow an identical pattern, in which two contrasting images are opposed. It would seem, in fact, that the cover illustrators of popular books had already discovered what would come to be known a few years later, in the era of political typo-photomontage, as 'dialectical montage'. Perfectly illustrating the official interpretations of the Tragic Week to which we referred above, we see here how the contraries are opposed didactically: the first of our examples simply shows the direct opposition of good and evil; in the second, the vision of destruction is countered by the reassuring vision of vigilant order: the 'force of order' immanent in the uniform, the rifle and the 'on guard' posture; in the third, the illegitimate violence of the 'seditious' gives way before the legitimate violence of the army and the State ...

Nothing could be clearer, then, albeit in the sense of 'nothing more obvious', or 'nothing more invisible', because on opening one of these books we are met by dozens of photographs of the destruction.

Certainly, some of these attempt the same type of discourse, of narrative in images, a kind of pathetic *biblia pauperum* of the fraudulent times of modernity: for example, in repetition, in publication after publication, of a photograph of a member of the Guardia Civil kneeling in front of another and tending to his wound, like a new version, all the more 'civil' for being more practically helpful, of the Biblical washing of the feet or some strange kind of Adoration of the Magi: the old history

Año IV — Barcelona, 10 Agosto de 1909 — Núm. 158

La Actualidad

Interior de la iglesia de las monjas Capuchinas de Manresa

15

Año IV — Barcelona, 28 Agosto de 1909

La Actualidad

Revista mundial de información gráfica

PUBLICACIÓN SEMANAL

Director: J. Roca y Roca

Redacción y Administración: Diputación, 344.—Teléfono 2108

RECUERDO DE BARCELONA

LA SEMANA TRÁGICA ANTE EL OBJETIVO FOTOGRÁFICO

Interior de la iglesia de las monjas Jerónimas, destruída por el incendio

Foto. Castellá

Número recopilación — 50 céntimos

RUINAS Y ESTRAGOS

Interior del colegio de Hermanas del Corazón de Jesús, sito en las calles de Grases y Virgen del Remedio (Pueblo Seco)

Iglesia antigua de Santa Madrona, sita en la calle de San Joaquín (Pueblo Seco) — Fotos. Castellá — Interior del convento de Paúles sito en la calle de Provenza, entre Muntaner y Aribau

CONVENTOS INCENDIADOS

Convento-colegio de Loreto, sito en la carretera de Sarriá, cuyo interior ha sufrido grandes desperfectos producidos por las llamas — Foto. Castellá

Entrada del convento de las monjas Carmelitas Gracia, dos horas después de entregado á las llamas — Foto. Camps

Restos del convento de Trinitarias, sito en la plaza de Blasco de Garay, del Pueblo Seco — Foto. Castellá

fig. 187, 188, 189, 190

fig. 191

LA BENEMÉRITA EN LOS ÚLTIMOS SUCESOS

Raimundo Pérez Martínez guardia mencionado con elogio en la orden del día de la plaza

Los dos guardias Pérez Martínez y García González, de la Comandancia de Cuenca, han sido mencionados con elogio en la orden del día de la plaza, por haber encontrado la suma de 5,400 pesetas pertenecientes á las monjas mínimas de Horta, y hecho entrega de dicha suma á la superioridad.—La primera cura de un guardia realizada por el teniente señor García Bueno patentiza el espíritu fraternal que reina en el cuerpo. —El cabo Prudencio Arjente Martínez, comandante del puesto de Caldas, concentrado en Sabadell, disfrazado de mozo de tren y burlando el cordón de vigilancia establecido por los rebeldes, después

Luis García González guardia mencionado con elogio en la orden del día de la plaza

Carro de la Guardia civil para facilitar el aprovisionamiento de muchas familias del Ensanche

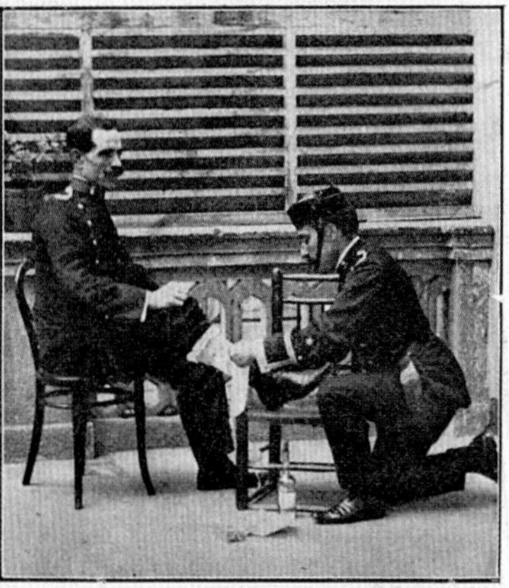

El teniente señor García Bueno, curando de primera intención al guardia Angel Feliu Camps herido cerca del Arco del Triunfo

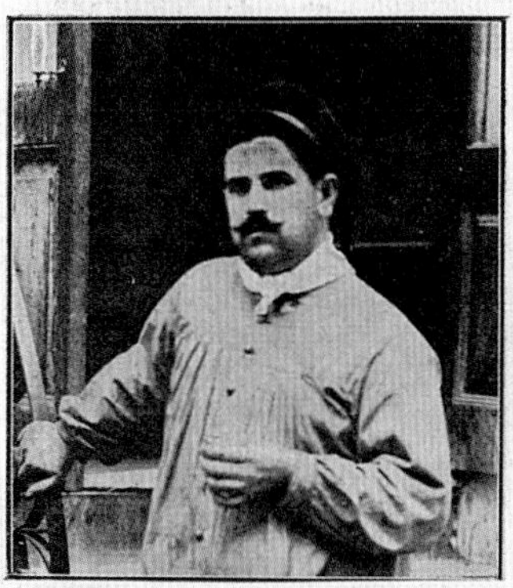

El cabo Prudencio Arjente Martínez que prestó un relevante servicio en Sabadell

de arrostrar mil peligros llegó á Barcelona participando á sus jefes lo comprometido de la situación.—El guardia Tomás López Fernández al trasladarse de Rubí á Manlleu, encontróse en Moncada con las líneas cortadas. Después de ocultarse entre la cintura el cerrojo del fusil dirigióse resueltamente á Barcelona. Un grupo de amotinados pretendió desarmarle y él dijo que otro grupo ya anteriormente le había quitado el cerrojo del máuser para impedir que hiciera fuego contra ellos. Gracias á esta estratagema pudo llegar á San Martín realizando actos de valor.

El guardia Tomás López Fernádez que con gran riesgo emprendió solo el viaje de Rubí á Barcelona

Fotos. Sánchez Carvajal

of art and its models here come to the aid of the meaning [fig. 191]. But the fact is that most of the pictures we find in the inside pages of those books, like those of the hundred A.T.V. postcards or the ones published in the illustrated press [fig. 187-191], are images that, if they were judged by the terms of the didactics-dialectics we have just commented on, would rank as terribly cryptic, silent, mute.

A good example of how disturbing photography's lack of eloquence can be is the impressive special edition that the weekly *La Actualidad* [fig. 188-191] published under the title 'Memento of Barcelona. The Tragic Week through the Camera Lens'.[82] The first part of the title—'Memento of Barcelona' ('Recuerdo de Barcelona')—places the hundred or so photographs of fires and destruction that fill its pages in the strange limbo not of the relic but of the *souvenir*: it seems the same path of trivialization must necessarily be trodden, between true destruction and its representation and photographic *publicizing*, that which is contained in the second part of the title: 'The Tragic Week through the Camera Lens'. The camera was, in fact, as these words tell us, still—objective, as always from now—in order for 'events' to pass through it.

In another postcard, this one not from the A.T.V. series, we see the ruins of the church of the Hieronymites: the floor is strewn with rubble and the vaults have collapsed, but the skeleton of the ribs hangs in a strange equilibrium, letting us see—as Maragall described in 'his' church—daylight through it, the daylight sharply outlining elements such as a surviving bell [fig. 192]. Two men, one a uniformed soldier with standard-issue rifle, have posed for the photographer. But in that 'dark light' the exposure time would have been too long, and they must have left before it finished and so appear on the plate as two transparent ghosts. On the other hand, the crowd milling at the door, no matter how much its members moved, remains a crowd: a mass, like the debris, 'through the camera lens'. Two equivalent modes, then, of 'making room', of clearing, like the merchandise that puts them in circulation.

The lens, then, far from the didactics-dialectics of order and disorder, of the legitimate and the illegitimate, proposes a new *a-legitimacy*: that of its own vacuity and its paratactic repetition. The Tragic Week postcards were collected and kept, in effect, as 'mementoes of Barcelona': could there be a better illustration for 'The Burned Church'? Photography of ruins and the void: this, then, is the new power of images: the artistic economy that inevitably emerged from the fire, hundreds of new images emerging—objectively and without paradox—from that iconoclasm. fig. 192

CONVENTOS INCENDIADOS
J.V. Nº 14 - BARCELONA - "GERONIMAS"

But let's return to our subject, by way of one of those photographs from the A.T.V. collection, No. 40: above the ruined church, just behind the cross that crowns its façade, which no one managed to pull down, we see the mass of the Sagrada Família, with the lower part of the four towers beginning to take shape [fig. 194]. The sharply pointed pinnacles of the apse rise up alongside the wooden scaffolding bristling from the stone, exaggerating the ambiguity of a construction that, behind the other, burned church, looks more than ever, as Maragall said, like destruction. Almost twenty years later, during the Spanish Civil War, *L'Esquella de la Torratxa* published a cartoon by Martí Bas[83] in which one character wonders why the arsonists have not vented their rage on the Sagrada Família, and another and another replying that it was because it wasn't yet finished [fig. 193]. It's a good answer, one that accords perfectly with the ideas of Pujols and the *needs* of the modern Barcelona: while on one hand churches burn and images are reduced to ashes, on the other those images grow and pile up on the giant bonfire of the Sagrada Família: a petrified bonfire, of course, like all 'collective dreams'. We should place next to the one hundred photographs of burned churches in the A.T.V. series the thousands of postcards that, from the beginning of its construction up to the present day, multiplying over and over like the Sagrada Família itself, have accompanied its growth and consolidated its tremendous power. The former next to the latter, and both interchangeably. But what else was the destiny, since long before, of this temple, but to be both the mirror and the depository of that overflow of images? [fig. 195, 196]

fig. 193

fig. 194

fig. 195, following pages fig. 196

Barcelona
La Sagrada Familia
BARCELONA
Caspe, 52.
Dr. Trenkler Co., Leipzig - Barcelona. No. 14480

Nº 177. BARCELONA
TEMPLO DE LA SAGRADA FAMILIA

Nº 115. BARCELONA
TEMPLO DE LA SAGRADA FAMILIA
ESPAÑA
5 CENT 5

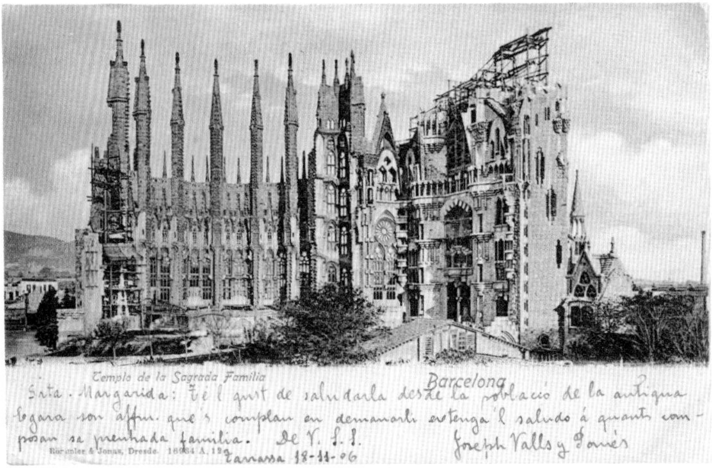
Templo de la Sagrada Familia
Barcelona
Srta. Margarida: Té'l gust de saludarla desde la població de la antigua Egara son affm. que's complau en demanarli estenga'l saludo á quants componsan sa prenhada familia. De V. S. S.
Joseph Valls y Tonés
Terrassa 18-11-06

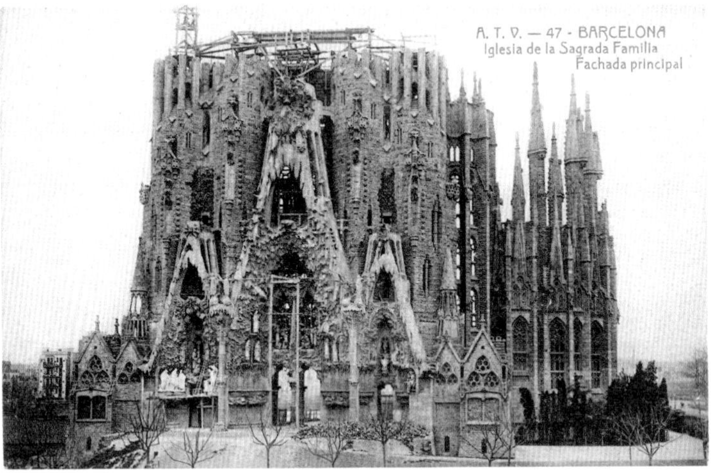
A. T. V. — 47 - BARCELONA
Iglesia de la Sagrada Familia
Fachada principal

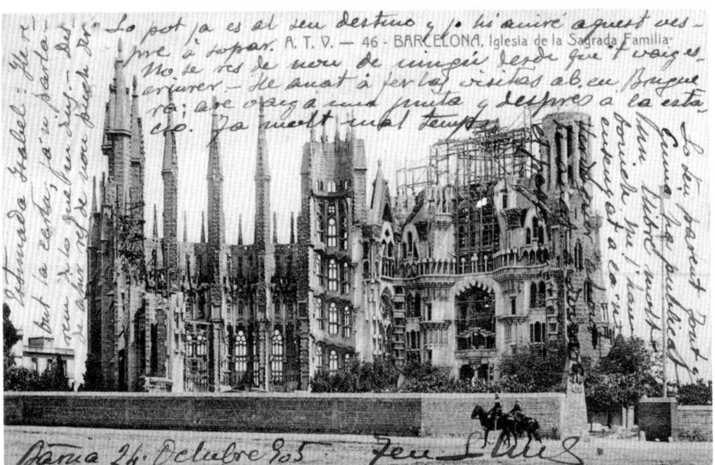
A. T. V. — 46 - BARCELONA. Iglesia de la Sagrada Familia

32 - Barcelona - Templo Sagrada Familia.
BYP

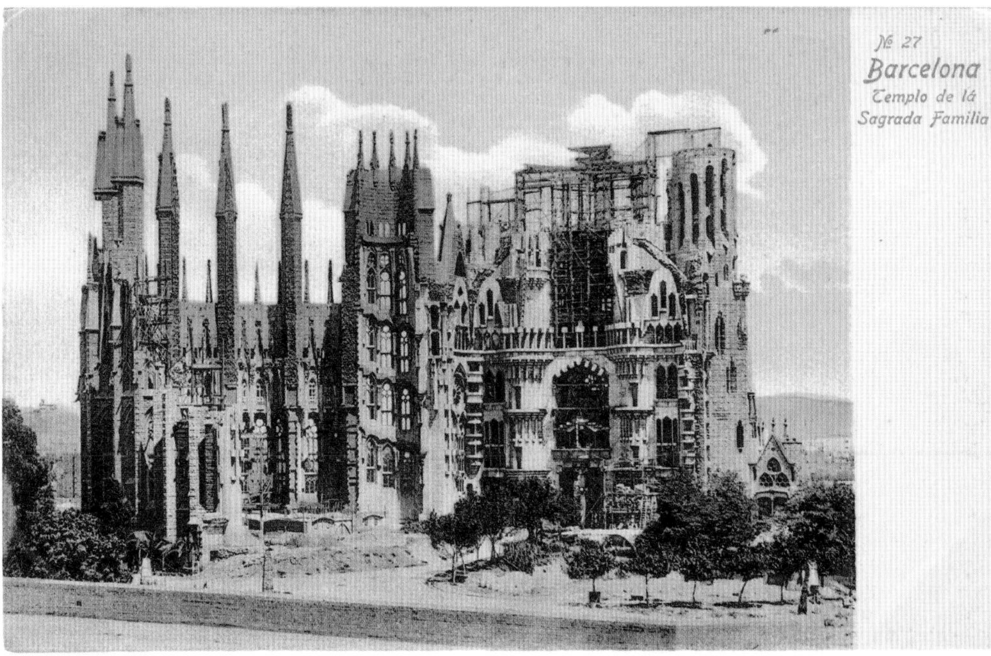
№ 27
Barcelona
Templo de lá
Sagrada Familia

BARCELONA. — Iglesia de la Sagrada Familia. — LL.

BARCELONA. 80 - Templo de la Sagrada familia
(Parte interior).

31 - Barcelona - Templo Sagrada Familia
B.Y.P.

N.º 9 – BARCELONA. Templo de la Sagrada Familia.
Vista general del Interior

N.º 7- BARCELONA. Templo expiatorio de la Sagrada Familia.
Vista general del exterior.

53 BARCELONA – TEMPLO DE LA SAGRADA FAMILIA

R. S. A.
101. BARCELONA. — Templo de la Sagrada Familia

BARCELONA - 20
PERSPECTIVA DE LA SAGRADA FAMILIA
PERSPECTIVA DE LA SAGRADE FAMILIA
PERSPECTIVE DE LA SAINTE FAMILLE

19 - BARCELONA - Templo de la Sagrada Familia en construcción.

1044 _ Barcelona _ Sagrada Familia .

BARCELONA - 29
TEMPLE DE LA SGDA. FAMILIA
TEMPLO DE LA SGDA. FAMILIA

The Temptation of Man

Let's take a small step back: a little more than ten years. In 1898 Joaquim Mir painted *The Cathedral of the Poor* [fig. 197]. In front of the Sagrada Família in construction it shows a group of beggars among the stones with which the temple is being built. Those stones that have not yet found their place in the construction are very white, and seem almost to be plaster or snow, with their blue shadows, or hallucinatory sugar — who knows what fancies may possess the hungry poor. The orange light of late afternoon warms the façade of the church. The beggars, however, are huddled in the shade. In the lower left corner we see the darkest of all, dressed in black and buried in a backlit darkness that seems to exist expressly for him. He is the *historicus*: he looks out at us and has let go of his crutch to hold out his hand for our charity. This is a young man, a boy, but Mir has endeavoured to concentrate in him all that is darkest in his picture, precisely that which from there, from below, from that corner on the left of the canvas, is absolutely opposed to the temple being warmed by the sun. Look at this boy, look at his broad, square jaw, at his broad red cheeks, at the prominence of the brow ridges, at the small eyes, at the large ears sticking out from the skull, at the low forehead, at his macrocephalism and the grimace of his mouth, which concludes the overall asymmetry of the face and head. It is not too difficult to see here all of the physical characteristics of the criminal, the degenerate so thoroughly described over twenty years before by Cesare Lombroso in *L'uomo delinquente* [fig. 202, 203], and before that by Galton and then by Bertillon, Bonomi, Anfosso and all the others, up to Max Nordau and beyond, each in his own way.[84]

fig. 197

Grup de mendicants que dema-
nàven almoina al portal d'entrada á la cripta els quals serviren
de model al pintor Mir pera el
seu cuadro "La catedral dels Pobres"

Foto presa cap el caient de la tarde poc
després d'haver plegat tothom de l'obra.

fig. 198, 199, 200

In any case, criminal anthropology, forensic science and art seem once again to be in agreement here as to the appearance of one of those atavistic types, as in many other things: down there in his backlit gloom, as the aforementioned authors state and illustrate, this beggar was born with the traits that define criminal, the savage or the ape. He reaches up to beg from the good bourgeois, the viewer of the picture, whom the picture itself tells that this is the same hand that could slit his throat. There he is now, in his darkness, stupefied, set apart from that imperfect holy family formed by the mother, the girls and the old people. A lad of working age but maimed, with outstretched open hand. What could that hand do if it had what it should not? Start a fire?

Doesn't that boy resemble, for example, some of the anarchists arrested in 1893 for the bombing of the Liceu Theater whom Santiago Rusiñol[85] sketched in his notes? They are grown men, of course, but the traits that served above to describe the boy would also hold for many of them. If we look at one of the folios [fig. 201] and set aside the older ones, whose long grey beards provoke a strange and unexpected feeling of respect, what do we see? The same asymmetrical skulls, the same bulging foreheads, the same small, widely spaced eyes, the same cheekbones, the same protruding ears. And then there are the expressions, fixed and fierce. Or the woman who appears in the centre: precisely because she is female, doubly threatening as a criminal and as a woman, the traits of wickedness seem if possible to be even more defiant: her mouth twitches in a scornful smile as she looks up at us with her pupils bulging like two hard, sharp carbuncles from the whites of her eyes and merging with the black shadow of thick eyebrows, her lower face darkened as if the artist were missing here the trace of an unkempt beard such as the other accused had (excessive hairiness was one of the things that, according to Lombroso and Ferrero, authors of *La donna delinquente*,[86] served to distinguish the degenerate woman): an impossible but necessary beard. And everything that Rusiñol sees in his models is just that: necessary. The criminal man, the female offender: these are the titles of Lombroso's books, the latter published in the same year that Rusiñol made these sketches. Drawn from life, though not from heads, whatever he and his public believed, but from a phenotype. Art itemizes for a fearful public the traits of innate criminality, or of class struggle, interchangeably. Let's take a look at another of those faces, the one on the right that Rusiñol marked with the number 18. We need only shave him to see our beggar boy. In other words, to see him grown to manhood and to see him in prison, at last accused of the crime for which he was born. It is him a few years later, necessarily.

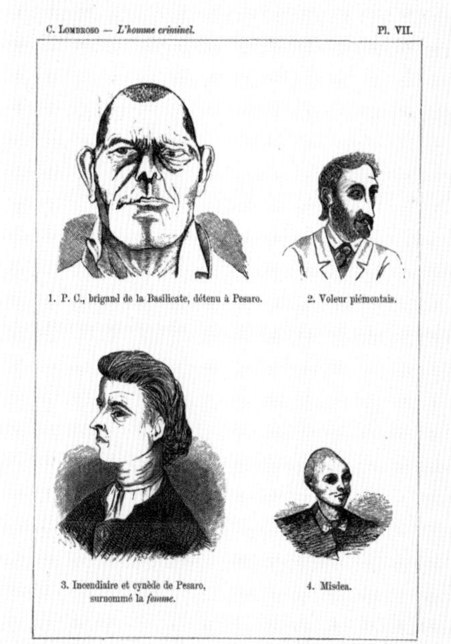

C. Lombroso — *L'homme criminel.*
Pl. VII.
1. P. C., brigand de la Basilicate, détenu à Pesaro.
2. Voleur piémontais.
3. Incendiaire et cynède de Pesaro, surnommé la *femme*.
4. Misdea.

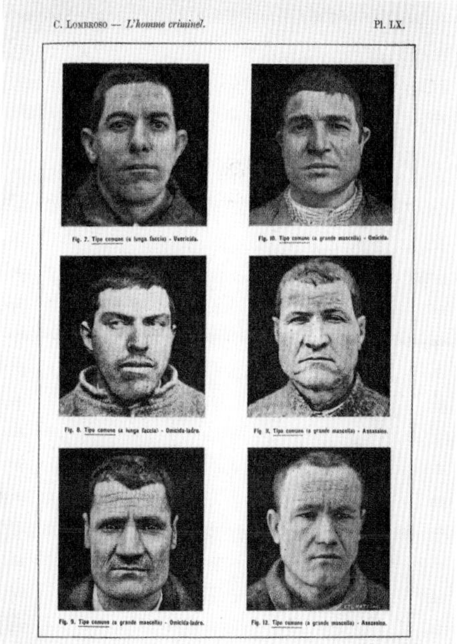

C. Lombroso — *L'homme criminel.*
Pl. LX.
Fig. 7. Tipo comune (a lunga faccia) - Uxoricida.
Fig. 10. Tipo comune (a grande mascella) - Omicida.
Fig. 8. Tipo comune (a lunga faccia) - Omicida-ladro.
Fig. 11. Tipo comune (a grande mascella) - Assassino.
Fig. 9. Tipo comune (a grande mascella) - Omicida-ladro.
Fig. 12. Tipo comune (a grande mascella) - Assassino.
TYPES DE CRIMINELS MEURTRIERS (Voir *Explication des planches*).

fig. 201, 202, 203

fig. 204, 205, 206

fig. 207

Leaving the Liceu on the night that Santiago Salvador[87] threw two bombs into the stalls of the theatre [fig. 204-206], November 7, 1893, Maragall wrote an extraordinary poem, of glacial lucidity.[88] It reads:

Furient va esclatant l'odi per la terra,
In frenzy erupts the hate for the land,
regalen sang les coll-torçades testes,
The broken-necked heads gushing blood,
i cal anâ a les festes
And one must go to a festivity
amb pit ben esforçat, com a la guerra.
With chest well out, as to war.

A cada esclat mortal—la gent trèmula es gira:
At each deadly outbreak—the trembling people turn:
la crudeltat que avança,—la por que s'enretira,
The cruelty that advances,—the fear that retreats,
se van partint el món...
Divide up the world ...
Mirant el fill que mama,—la mare que sospira,
Watching the child at the breast,—the mother that sighs,
el pare arruga el front.
The father frowns.

Pro l'infant innocent,
But the innocent child
que deixa, satisfet, la buidada mamella,
That turns away, satisfied, from the emptied breast,
se mira an ell,—se mira an ella,
Looks on him,—looks on her,
i riu bàrbarament.
and laughs barbarously.

The first line identifies, as we should expect, the explosion of the bomb with the eruption of hatred, the shock wave of one with the spreading of the other; it is generic, conventional, and thus contrasts more violently—and violence *also* has to emerge from the poem in the form of a lump in the throat—with the very concrete truculence of the second, bloody line in which a ferocious, synthetic expression, 'broken-necked heads', places before our eyes the terrible image of people killed instantly, their torsos still upright, supported by the backs of the theatre seats and now suddenly lifeless, and of heads hanging from broken necks. But Maragall is leaving the opera [fig. 207], no doubt in black and white, in evening dress, white tie, top hat and silk scarf, and as a member of his class he cannot avoid a new contrast in the following couplet, this time ironic, deriving from the detachment to be maintained in the presence of horror by a true gentleman, always impassive, whose exquisite sang-froid, whose *sprezzatura,* makes him take the hardest course for the easiest, whether at a social gathering or on the battlefield, at a festive occasion or in the midst of horror. The next three lines, conventional once again, are a gloss on the first, a reiteration in which the first line effectively develops into action; above all, they mark a pause, a brief respite that disarms the reader and sends her unsuspecting into the last six lines, which pour out in a swift and terrible crescendo, from the verses in the second stanza depicting the mother nursing her child and the pensive father, fearful of the future, like a pious image of the holy family, to the four lines of the last stanza, in which the satisfaction of the infant is starkly juxtaposed with the empty breast and, even more terribly, its innocence—that of a baby at its mother's breast: nothing could be more ingenuously reassuring—is contrasted with the laughter of the sinister last line and the last word with its ante-antepenultimate stress: 'barbarously'. If, as we said, Rusiñol and Mir identified for their public, which was the public of a Liceu turned into a battlefield, the hereditary traits of the criminal, Maragall describes—in its mother's lap, in its nest—the infant and its food. He it is who will reach out to beg. Holy family, *unheimlich.* That poem in which the penultimate line the child, before laughing, looks at its parents as in a mirror, is entitled—barbarously, of course—'Paternal': and of what does it speak but the serpent's egg?

Well, then: the serpent coils down from a corbel on the right side of the Rosary Chapel of the Sagrada Família [fig. 213], construction of which began in 1894, followed by its decoration in 1897. In other words, it began to be built just after the Liceu bombs and to be decorated the year after the bombing of the Corpus Christi procession outside the church of Santa Maria del Mar.

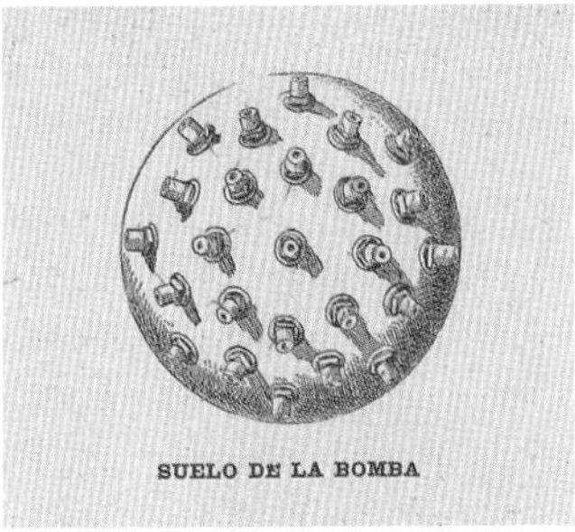

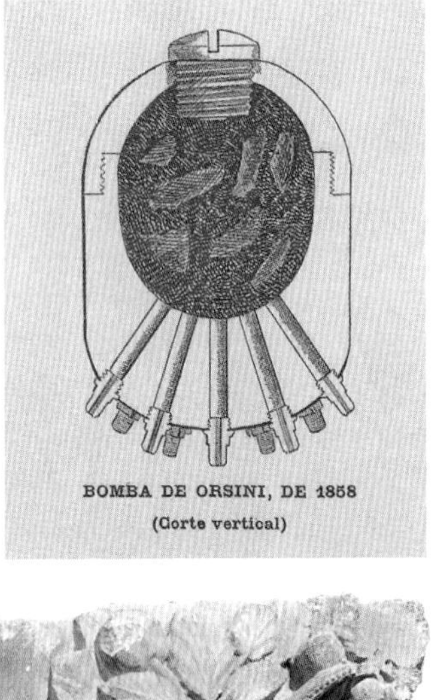

fig. 208, 209, 210, 211

fig. 212

The attacks that marked the two climactic moments of terror, shock and repression in the decade in which Barcelona was, precisely, 'the city of the bombs' thus initiate two phases of work on the Rosary Chapel. The serpent slithers at the same height as the twining rose bushes and coils round the very branches from which fall the petals of the promised shower of roses that decorates the whole chapel. Serpent or dragon or demon. We see its fibrous ringed body twist in the air as it clings to the wall with the sharply pointed claws of its long bony talons. Its head is deformed, tremendously tapered, literally receding—as is the way with serpents. It is, in fact, a strange anamorphosis of a human head, but not of any human head: gigantic skull, pronounced brow ridges, slanted eyes, prominent cheekbones ... Why go on describing the modern demon when we know that the monsters are here among us? The features are tensed like the muscles and swollen like the veins of a neck in the extreme effort of a scream that won't come, that will be no more than a whisper or a long shrill whistle, as sharp as the head itself. Actually, that scream will sound forth in another scream, that of the man the demon hangs over, who also stretches, with all his might, his short neck, his hand lifted to a mouth twisted into a grimace. But I will not talk about his large ear, which is not only an atavistic trait of criminality and degeneracy but also, as if that were not enough, seems to say to the demon: 'the better to hear you with!' And the demon could answer the man with the same story if he were to ask about his immense mouth, which eats, swallows and, especially, speaks for itself, or about the claw that gives, that bestows. From behind his back, then, this man in smock and rope-soled sandals, this worker is receiving from the demon, in his left hand, a bomb [fig. 212]. So is original sin represented now: the temptation of Eve is the man's temptation, and the apple, the fruit that had let loose all earthly desires is a metal sphere, an industrially produced infernal mechanism placed in the hand of the have-not, a fatal expedient not now at the beginning of life but at the end of production [fig. 208-210]. There are very few depictions of Eve receiving the fruit from behind, without looking, like this worker. But there is at least one, and it is truly glorious: it was carved by Gislebertus on a lintel of the north portal of the Cathedral of Saint Lazare in Autun, in or around 1130 [fig. 211]. Prone on the ground among the trees of paradise, Eve rests on her knees and right elbow; her left hand is stretched behind her to pluck the apple, but her head is raised and her eyes look far in front of her, and she holds the open palm of her right hand to her mouth, perhaps to support her cheek or, better, as if about to cry out, to call to Adam, who is missing from the scene, probably in the other half of a bas-relief of which we only know this fragment. fig. 213

UNA MARAVILLA DEL CLAUSTRO

BARCELONA. — CLAUSTRO DEL TEMPLO DE LA SAGRADA FAMILIA. PUERTA DE LA VIRGEN DEL ROSARIO, VERDADERA MARAVILLA DE PIEDRA EN LA QUE PUSO GAUDÍ TODAS LAS PERFECCIONES DE SU GENIO INNOVADOR Y DE SU TÉCNICA NO IGUALADA EN NINGUNA OBRA MODERNA.

(Foto Zerkowitz)

fig. 214

fig. 215, 216

Eve kneels and falls gracefully forward to fill the whole of the lintel's horizontal format, just as the worker in the smock crouches to become a compact corbel; both cry out, Eve before tasting the apple, the worker before throwing the bomb. In neither case does the right hand know what the left is doing. Autun was a stage on the pilgrimage to Santiago, and pilgrims who stopped in front of the cathedral would have been moved by the Last Judgement on the tympanum, sculpted and proudly signed by Gislebertus at the feet of Christ. The north front was dedicated to the Fall of Man, and it is there that we see the beautiful Eve with her long flowing hair stretched naked among the plants, one of which—perhaps the Tree of Life—caresses her belly. Eve herself was the temptation: she was the serpent and what came out of the apple. The bas-relief on the Autun portal was removed, but in the corbel on the Sagrada Família, which is next to the portal of the Nativity façade that was now—then, at the end of the nineteenth century—being built, the gestures were repeated, the woman replaced by the worker, the apple replaced by the bomb, as if in a modern farce: a clockwork apple.

Just as the *naturalism* of the roses in the Rosary Chapel is exaggerated, so too is that of the bomb the worker receives in his left hand, although in this case, of course, naturalism is not quite the word. That bomb is, in the strictest sense, hyperrealist, the product of the same delirious *Sachlichkeit* from which many Lombrosian heads sprouted: an Orsini bomb like the one Santiago Salvador threw into the audience at the Liceu leaving a final toll of some twenty people dead and almost forty more wounded. But in fact, as we know, he actually threw two bombs. The first exploded on hitting the back of a seat in row—alas!—thirteen; the second, so say the most pious legends, landed in the lap of a woman who was already dead and did not explode. Two bombs that were etched forever in the imaginary of Barcelona not only because they were an attack on the cream of society in the very heart of its theatre, in the exact scenario—the stalls, the boxes, the five balconies—in which important gentlemen ritually represented the splendour of their business and the order and hierarchy of society through the exhibition of their families—half of the victims were women, as the period press was at great pains to point out, with lurid descriptions of their rich gowns drenched with blood—but also because one of the bombs did not explode: that is to say, it remained there, in their midst, the strangest cyst, a sign of some unspeakable disease, metal from the hand of the anarchist, a ball of fire in opaque metal, power converted forever into a real object, actual, an exaggerated thing among everyday things, an infamous legacy to bear, a sphere that occupied space and could only be approached with fear. The bomb that did not explode is the sacred image we cannot look away from, or the enigmatic fetish, sinister to the point of suffocation; it is the idol that the meteorite fallen from the sky into the midst of the tribe necessarily becomes; the black stone that grips us and terrifies us because we all know what it contains: the immense power and energy of a vengeful and capricious god...and at the same time nothing, absolutely nothing, because—and this we both know and do not know—is in its perfect emptiness that its terrible power lies. That iron ball, gleaming, bristling, will end up being gazed upon with awe and admiration in the display case of the Museum of the History of Barcelona, like the relic of some extraterrestrial message bearing tremendous warnings [fig. 208]. The cream of Barcelona society could fit into a horseshoe, the horseshoe of their theatre, now transformed into an amphitheatre of wild beasts. That space was a small and compact, like the bomb that had become its most perfect and most terrible image.

For years afterwards, the chronicles say, the people in the stalls of the Liceu would look cautiously up, and leave a large swathe of empty seats around the place where the bomb had gone off: the truth is that those empty seats were perennially occupied by another bomb, the one that did not explode, as if it were still there, embedded or buried, and exercised around itself a strange centripetal force.

In the photograph of the execution of Santiago Salvador, carried out a year later in the yard of the prison on carrer Santa Amàlia, something similar but perfectly symmetrical, centrifugal, occurs [fig. 215]. In the foreground we see an orderly group of soldiers, their backs to a wall, their uniforms repeating the same dark silhouette adorned by the same white collars and the same caps. In the middle of the picture the public is concentrated in a ring around the scaffold on which the condemned man is being garrotted. Between the two groups is a deeply disturbing, exasperating empty space whose hard, smooth surface looks like the great bare wall of the prison thrown down, flattened. The gas lamps and the trees, also planted in the void, become signs of absence and devastation. On the right a black trunk leans at the same angle as the rails of the stair at the back of the scaffold. In this photo there is none of the movement we see in *Garrote vil*, painted by Ramon Casas in the same year, which depicts another execution, that of Aniceto Peinador, in the same place [fig. 214]. Here the hats move and the necks stretch, the horses come and go, the trees are masts for the crowd and a portico for the soldiers, while the gap between the public and the scaffold has been occupied by the most solemn and remarkable persons and objects: the banner, the image of the crucifixion, the priests, the pointed hoods ... The painting was intended, as has often been said, to be a chronicle or document of that execution, but in a stricter sense it could be called its story; the photograph, in contrast, shows nothing but a gelid trace: that terrible void. On what other plot could the expiatory, hyperrealist temple be raised? What other open space will its images overflow?

It cannot have been very difficult for Maragall to call his poem 'Paternal', nor for the devil to replace an apple with a bomb. A slip would suffice. After all, the bomb attack in the Liceu took place during the second act of Rossini's *Guillaume Tell*. The father's hand does not tremble when he has to shoot the arrow at the apple resting on his son's head. I am not surprised that many years later an admirer of Gaudí, Dalí, should make William Tell the image of the father in his own version of the Oedipus myth. In 1931, in *Dalí ou l'anti-obscurantisme*, René Crevel compared him to Abraham sacrificing Isaac, or God the father sacrificing Christ.[89] And I find it even less surprising that in 1933, in *L'Énigme de Guillaume Tell* [fig. 217], one of the most absurd pictures Dalí ever painted, giant like the old history paintings, as banal as most of them, that paternal patriotic hero should have the face of Lenin [fig. 218]. He squints at us and laughs, as he does in the last photographs of him, or as he did at his last public appearance, in which 'he wanted to speak, but was no longer able to articulate words; it was impossible to understand him. They all listened to him in silence. Finally he stopped and ... began to laugh, to laugh wildly.'[90] His smile tells us, no doubt, as William Tell told his son in the scene with the apple that Wagner liked so much, 'Stay still!'. We shall see that it was no joke.

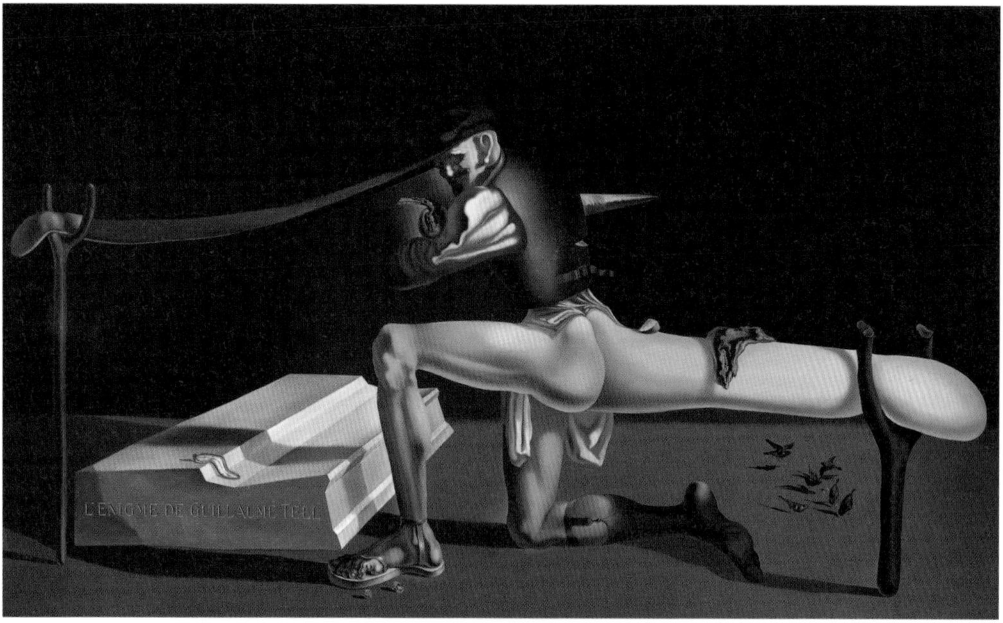

fig. 217

fig. 218

'Immortal Ruins'

In the last lines of the *prière d'insérer* that Breton and Éluard wrote for *La Femme visible*, the book by Salvador Dalí published by Editions Surréalistes in 1930, we read: 'paranoiac-critical thinking is the most remarkable instrument that has ever been proposed for passing through the immortal ruins the ghost-woman with the grey-green face, the laughing eye and the hard curls who is not only the spirit of our birth, that is to say of the *modern style* but the increasingly captivating ghost of *becoming*.'[91]

We shall not discuss here how Breton and Éluard attempt to relate the Dalinian method to the dialectical thinking that was so dear to both of them, especially at this time; nor, for now, the specific *bibelot* [fig. 219] to which the description of the ghost-woman corresponds (clearly one of those languid female busts that were among the great aesthetic—and not only aesthetic—obsessions of Art Nouveau) but insist instead on something probably more important and less circumstantial: on the fact that, for them, Dalí appears literally to be the discoverer of the *modern style*, and even more on all the things that are associated with the *modern style* here, such as the ruins, the spirit of *their* infancy, and becoming, that power of being.

Breton and Éluard are really speaking of a kind of eternity of yesterday, of a time that is anachronistic or, more precisely, retrospective, which nevertheless appears embedded in the present, set hard like those curls, turned to stone, mineralized.

When in his paintings or in the texts of *La Femme visible* Dalí focuses on that architecture, that sculpture and those Art Nouveau objects he is placing before the eyes of our pair of surrealists a world of forms, or a world of *things*, that were thought to be dead and buried, belonging to a far distant period with which the people and the tastes of the early nineteen thirties could in no way be identified or which, more precisely, could only be seen as reflecting the more than dubious vagaries of their grandparents' taste and a *fin de siècle* absolutely superseded by the war, revolutions, machinist productivism, the avant-gardes and 'contemporary lyricism' as not only *past* but ridiculous and contemptible. Now suddenly these ornamental objects that had been expelled from the interiors of the bourgeois home and bourgeois life as *démodé* junk, deserving at most a smile of condescension, were regarded as something that was still there, on all sides, as a sediment or residue—that far from belonging to a remote past, as *modern* taste or good taste had endeavoured to believe or to make believe—but was barely thirty years old, more or less same age as our protagonists. Prehistory, then, was what emerged with them in the present, though free, of course, of nostalgia and of utopias of resurrection, as the simple realization that the most distant past was *still* there, visible in its detritus, close at hand: the detritus of a life not yet very long, the detritus of their own childhood.

The time, then, was contracted into a kind of palaeontological restoration of yesterday: that architecture and those objects that had been the whole world just thirty years before, now abandoned by the world, were struggling to emerge in the present or in everyday life as shells not only empty but petrified, as authentic fossils. However, what was revealed by the *study* of those fossils was not the customs of ancestors who peopled the earth in a remote time—our grandparents and parents—but our own lives, suspended in them.

Breton and Éluard speak of 'immortal ruins,' but that is merely a comfortingly *poetic* way of saying that all those objects are nothing but the *hollow* form of the present. Childhood returns as a ghost, converted into *becoming*, that *being able to be* nothing more than attractive, but the truth is that childhood never left us: how else are we to explain the characteristic retrospective and repetitive rhythm of modernity?

There is still more to be said about the words of Breton and Éluard. In fact, this architecture and these *modern style* objects were simply the image that the bourgeoisie—which created them—had given itself: a metaphor, comforting as

fig. 219, 220

metaphor always is, of their dominion over nature and technique, the *mechanics* of the latter subjected to the *form* of the former—objects ignorant, as such, of 'the physics of the plastic';[92] and they were also quite clearly the interpretation of progress and of the taste associated with that progress through which the bourgeoisie sought to make the masses identify with their own objectives. So the *world* that has abandoned those objects is none other than that of the bourgeoisie's *aspirations*, leaving them buried like fossils in a far from distant prehistory, so close that they still form part not of the taste but of the 'unconscious of the masses'—which should be called by *its* name: alienation—that undoubtedly identified with them, though we could say better: identified it with them.

As the bourgeoisie began to abandon the *modern style*, it became the popular style *par excellence*: in other words, *kitsch*, which is a word co-opted to distinguish the 'authentic' but now past from its present and accessible 'copies' in an age when the increasingly numerous middle classes began to consume the vast output of goods produced expressly for them in order to turn them into consumers or the first product of consumption itself: furniture, figurines, bagatelles, *bibelots* and knick-knacks of all kinds, all *cheap*. The *modern style* became cheaper, it was remaindered, and in the eyes of our poets and artists, our surrealists—the latest and supremely decanted examples of the anarcho-aristocratizing intellectual so characteristic of that *fin de siècle*—how could those forms *return*—of course: it's a way of speaking—but as *dream*, or, more accurately, as nightmare or delirium, as they said? What, indeed, was the thing they called the 'collective dream' but the ultimate effect of an 'infantile neurosis'?

In the late nineteen twenties, when Dalí arrived in Paris, Art Nouveau was already a far distant thing there, or at least so it seems to be in the opinion of those who for one reason or another, from 'contemporary lyricism' or simply from cosmopolitan 'good taste'—and always, in every case, from a 'new need'—referred to it. To give some symmetrical examples: Henri Verne and René Chavance, in their guide *Pour comprendre l'art moderne décoratif en France*, published in 1925 on the occasion of the International Exposition of Modern Industrial and Decorative Arts, entitled a highly condescending previous chapter 'The 1900 Error';[93] Le Corbusier, at the beginning of an important article of 1927, 'Où en est l'architecture?', wrote no less condescendingly of the style of the little flowers of St Francis and the 'boneless architecture' of the turn of the century;[94] Christian Zervos, in *Cahiers d'Art* in 1929, reviewing Ràfols and Folguera's book on Gaudí (the first monograph study of his work), spoke of absurdity, aberration, a cocktail of styles, the looting of history and an architecture that 'would scarcely merit a modest mention in a catalogue of curiosities',[95] and Paul Morand in 1931, in his book *1900*, denounced a style that 'infected' everything and, in the era of light and electricity, allowed 'the poisonous' to triumph.[96]

But if Paris, capital of the luxury markets and of the most expensive of these, the art market, had logically agreed to repudiate Art Nouveau—and, given the emergence of a cultural mass market, it is not difficult to imagine the motive for this *belated* insistence on its anachronism and the 'bad taste' attributed to it—that was not the case in Barcelona. Certainly, the *Noucentistes* here attacked *Modernisme* with the same intransigence as the Parisians we have just mentioned, and need not recall the campaigns at the end of the twenties, led by Manuel Brunet, calling for the Palau de la Música Catalana in Barcelona to be demolished and replaced by a modern 'Salle Pleyel' or the lamentations of Carles Soldevila, who in his guidebook *L'art d'ensenyar Barcelona* (The Art of Showing Barcelona), published in 1929,[97] complained that there was no alternative but to show visitors precisely what should be hidden but everyone wanted to see: the Milà house, the Sagrada Família and the other Gaudí buildings, which, as could be read in the Baedecker guides and the travel books, from Morand to Carco by way of many others, had given the city an ambiguous and irksome fame, that was between plain vulgarity and inspired eccentricity, between *kitsch* and naïf.[98]

But of course, in contrast to Paris, in Barcelona at the end of the twenties *Modernisme* still pervaded everything: Gaudí had died in 1926 a mythic architect—his funeral was an apotheosis [fig. 221]—with a gigantic building under construction; excessive in every way, its anachronism oiling the sentimental cogs both of the Church and of conservative Catalanism, that building was still being incessantly apostrophized in books, newspapers and magazines as Barcelona's new cathedral: that is to say, the city's *collective work*, funded by donations, before which the *Noucentistes* bowed down unconditionally, recognizing its political and ideological usefulness and sometimes even seeing in its delusional forms the order of a Greek temple (as Folch i Torres was inspired to do).[99]

following pages fig. 221

There is an unexpected interpretation of that anachronistic and sentimental—in other words, interested and political—persistence of *Modernisme* in Barcelona in the late twenties in a pamphlet that Francesc Pujols published in 1927, when Dalí was writing his first articles for *L'Amic de les Arts*, entitled, as we know, *La visió artística i religiosa d'en Gaudí* (The Artistic and Religious Vision of Gaudí).

Barcelona :: Entierro del ilustre arquitect

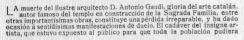

El ilustre arquitecto catalán D. Antonio Gaudí, muerto recientemente á consecuencia de haber sido atropellado por un tranvía. Último retrato del gran artista obtenido en la procesión del Corpus, por Merletti

LA muerte del ilustre arquitecto D. Antonio Gaudí, gloria del arte catalán, autor famoso del templo en construcción de la Sagrada Familia, entre otras importantísimas obras, constituye una pérdida irreparable, y ha dado ocasión á sentidísimas manifestaciones de duelo. El cadáver del insigne artista, que estuvo expuesto al público para que toda la población pudiera

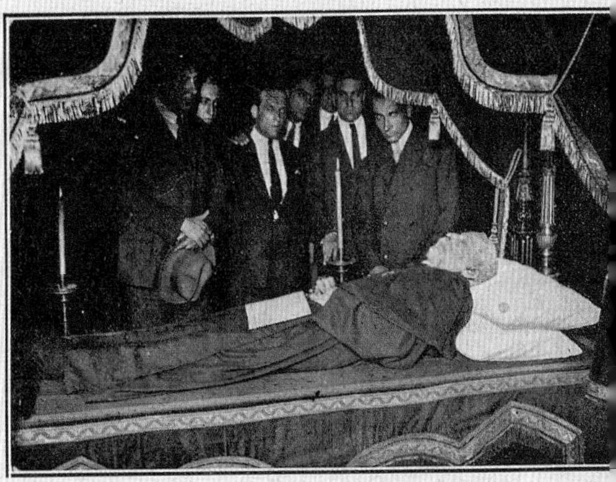

El cadáver del ilustre arquitecto D. Antonio Gaudí, en la capilla ardiente del Hospi Santa Cruz, donde estuvo expuesto al público Fot. Pérez

Momento de sacar del carro fúnebre el cadáver del Sr. Gaudí, ante el templo de la Familia, en el que recibió sepultura

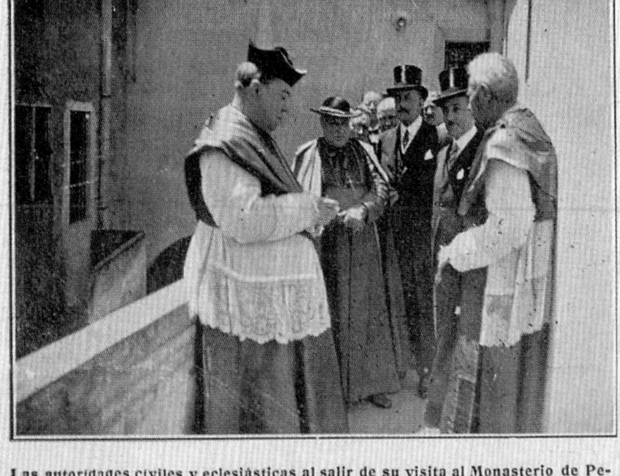

Las autoridades civiles y eclesiásticas al salir de su visita al Monasterio de Pedralbes, el día 13 del corriente Fot. Merletti

Las autoridades civiles, militares y universitarias en la procesión de la de Caridad, efectuada solemnemente Fots. Pérez d

. Antonio Gaudi, y otras notas de actualidad

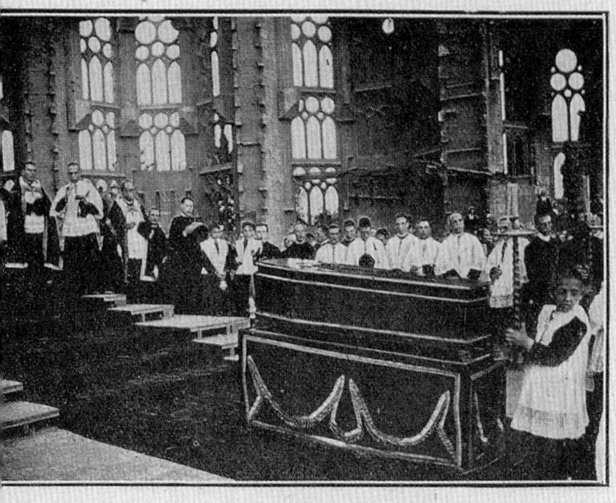

ro barcelonés cantando responsos ante el cadáver del Sr. Gaudi, al llegar al templo de la Sagrada Familia, obra del insigne arquitecto, donde recibió sepultura

nitiva fúnebre que acompañó el cadáver del Sr. Gaudi, en imponente manifestación de duelo, entrando en el templo de la Sagrada Familia Fots. Merletti

Estado actual de las obras del templo de la Sagrada Familia, obra sobresaliente del insigne arquitecto D. Antonio Gaudi, gloria del arte catalán

rendir á la memoria del maestro el tributo debido, recibió después cristiana sepultura en la cripta del templo cuya construcción dirigía el incomparable arquitecto, cuyas obras dieron una personalidad indiscutible y han de perpetuar su nombre. Nosotros nos asociamos de todo corazón al duelo general por la muerte de tan exclarecido artífice.

lejandro Lerroux con los organizadores del homenaje que se le tributó en la Casa del Pueblo, Sres. Iglesias, Vinaixa, Pérez de Rozas Roure y Olivella

La embarcación "Lola", que obtuvo el primer premio en las regatas del Campeonato Internacional de Cataluña Fot. Merlett

Rather than entering here into the main theme of the Pujols text, centred on Catalonia's mission to put an end to Catholicism and replace it with the true religion (about which, it must be said, he goes into very little detail), we will do better to recall the role to be played by Gaudí's temple. Let's go back to that quote from Pujols: '...it is the case with those that, raising pigs for slaughter, give them all they can to fatten them so that weigh what they ought to when the day comes to sacrifice them [...] and everyone knows that no part of the pig goes to waste.'[100] The brutality of the Pujols metaphor lies in the fact that, unlike the comparisons with the pâtisserie so common in speaking of Art Nouveau architecture, it contains no reference to aesthetic taste but is appeals wholly and directly to another kind of taste, essentially cannibal and manifestly political, to the taste buds of politics, so that Gaudí's religious architecture becomes an object not of devotion but of devouring. Gaudí's work therefore feeds that great, immense, *eternal* body, a dying Catholicism; it is an *edible* architecture, edible in its entirety because, like the pig, no part of it goes to waste.

There is no need to read Dalí's Parisian writings of the early thirties very closely to appreciate how this ferocious metaphor, arising directly from the sentimental dregs and residue of *Modernisme* and its anachronistic persistence yet at the same time a sinister image of the eternity of yesterday, a bestial transcendence of any idea of beauty or ugliness, elaborated in the depths of the most absolute fetishism, was to become the mainstay of his championing of the *modern style* in general and of Gaudí in particular; that is to say, the metaphor into which he would plunge his hands. In the 'spirit' of Dalí's birth, in the spirit of his childhood there lies sleeping, then, the monster that that metaphor awakens, a 'terrifying and edible' architecture. But that metaphor is not alone.

Already in Paris in 1929, the year of *Un Chien Andalou* and his first exhibition at the Galerie Goemans, Dalí had read three of the entries in the 'Dictionnaire critique' (Critical Dictionary) that was being published in *Documents*, all by Bataille. In the first, 'Architecture', published in issue No. 2,[101] he speaks of architecture as the great metaphor of order and of authority, that in which the face of power is directly reflected and that which reduces man to an intermediate link in the evolution from ape to architecture, whose monuments inspire not only 'social wisdom' but 'often even real fear', and finally proposes 'bestial monstrosity' as the only way of escaping the 'architectural mob'; in the other two entries, 'Abattoir' and 'Cheminée d'usine', both of which appeared in issue No. 6,[102] Bataille gives two specific examples of this architecture: one, the slaughterhouse, hidden away out of sight in modern societies in which blood no longer mixes with cocktails, and whose curse 'terrifies only those who utter it', who are 'reduced to eating cheese'; the other, the factory chimney, the subject of 'chlorotic admiration' of the 'truly wretched aesthetes' of today, and whose 'lugubrious filth', however, comes from the memories of 'early childhood' of 'our generation' as the paradigm form of a 'terrifying architecture', worse than that of 'even the most monstrous' churches.

Here again there is little need—and perhaps even less than before—to pay much attention to Dalí's texts to perceive the influence of Bataille's dictionary entries. As is well known, Dalí had been an object of attention in *Documents* on a number of occasions in that year of 1929: in issue No. 4, under the dictionary entry 'Œil', precisely, and the by no means fortuitous title 'Friandise cannibale',[103] Bataille had lavished praise on *Un Chien Andalou*, which 'penetrates so deeply into the horror' as to enthral the viewer as an adventure film would, and had published a reproduction of *Le miel est plus doux que le sang*; a little further on, on a page of illustrations dedicated to the phenomenon of anamorphosis, we find two more paintings by Dalí, *Baigneuses* and *Nu féminin*, making *Documents* the first French magazine to take an interest in the artist's work; finally, issue No. 7 carried an important piece by Bataille entitled 'Le jeu lugubre':[104] here a reproduction of the painting of the same name had to be replaced by a diagram because Dalí, who had aligned himself completely with Breton, asked the Viscount de Noailles, who owned the picture, to refuse *Documents* permission to use it [fig. 222] .

'Le jeu lugubre' appeared in December 1929; in July 1930, in the first issue of Breton's new magazine *Le Surréalisme au service de la Révolution*, Dalí published his first article in Paris, 'L'âne pourri',[105] which is essential reading for two reasons: the first, and the one we shall consider now, is that here Dalí clearly defined the method that came to be known as paranoiac-critical; the second is because it sets out for the first time his defence of *modern style* architecture, held up as a paradigmatic example of the 'great simulacrum' that the paranoiac-critical method proposed. What is more, Dalí also mentions Bataille in this piece, in a footnote in which—following the line indicated by Breton, who had called Bataille an 'anti-dialectical materialist'—he accuses him of being an 'old materialist'. That said, we need only consider Dalí's arguments or take a look at his paintings to concur with what has been said many times before, namely that this is an absolutely rhetorical or political accusation: however much Breton and Éluard strove—and we have seen how they did—to enlist Dalí in their ranks, those of the dialectic, or more precisely, of Romantic idealism, could any materialism be more anti-dialectical than his?

But that political footnote attacking Bataille was more than a gesture towards Breton and his friends; quite clearly Dalí was attempting here to mark his distance from what was the main and most obvious influence on a number of key aspects of his text.

'Architecture' saw the light—a figure of speech, of course—in May 1929; just one year before, in May 1928, *L'Amic de les Arts* had published the text of Dalí's talk at the meeting in Sitges together with a 'Note'—though this was eliminated, incidentally, from subsequent editions—in which he declared himself, in rather excited language, the firmest admirer of Le Corbusier—whom he paraphrased in such titles as 'Photography, Pure Creation of the Spirit', among other things, and whose influence continues to be evident in important aspects of 'La dada fotogràfica' (The photographic datum) in 1929—[106] and described the architect as 'the most hygienic spirit of our age', as well as dedicating the text to him.

Now, what is the 'architectural composition' that Bataille puts forward as the perfect metaphor of the social order and the physiognomy of power but harmony, rhythm, lyricism, 'regulating lines', the 'Doric morality' or any of the images with which Le Corbusier defined architecture, which is itself an image, of course, of its society, and led him to conclude his *Vers une architecture* with the famous question 'Architecture or Revolution?', the answer to which is 'Revolution can be avoided'?[107] And isn't it in order to give the world 'architecture' in place of 'revolution' that Le Corbusier, like those 'truly wretched aesthetes' of whom Bataille speaks, admires the factories and smokestacks whose productivist perfection he legitimizes through the comparison with classical architecture and particularly with San Pietro and the Parthenon, 'pure creation of the spirit', and also, at the end of the day, like the work of Michelangelo, a temple?

Bataille's texts obviously contain the keys to Dalí's new insight: when he says in 'L'âne pourri' that the *modern style* is everything that should be opposed to the 'defenders of the execrable "modern art"' and to 'our swinish contemporary aestheticians', to whom should we refer such expressions? Well-chosen expressions, without a doubt, in that they play an essential role in the characterization of this 'pure and disturbing' architecture that only a few years later, in 1933, in *Minotaure*, will have become 'terrifying and edible' [fig. 107].[108]

When Dalí speaks of the 'cold and intoxicating' buildings of *modern style* architecture as being 'enough, too, to confound the whole history of art'[109] we are still fig. 222

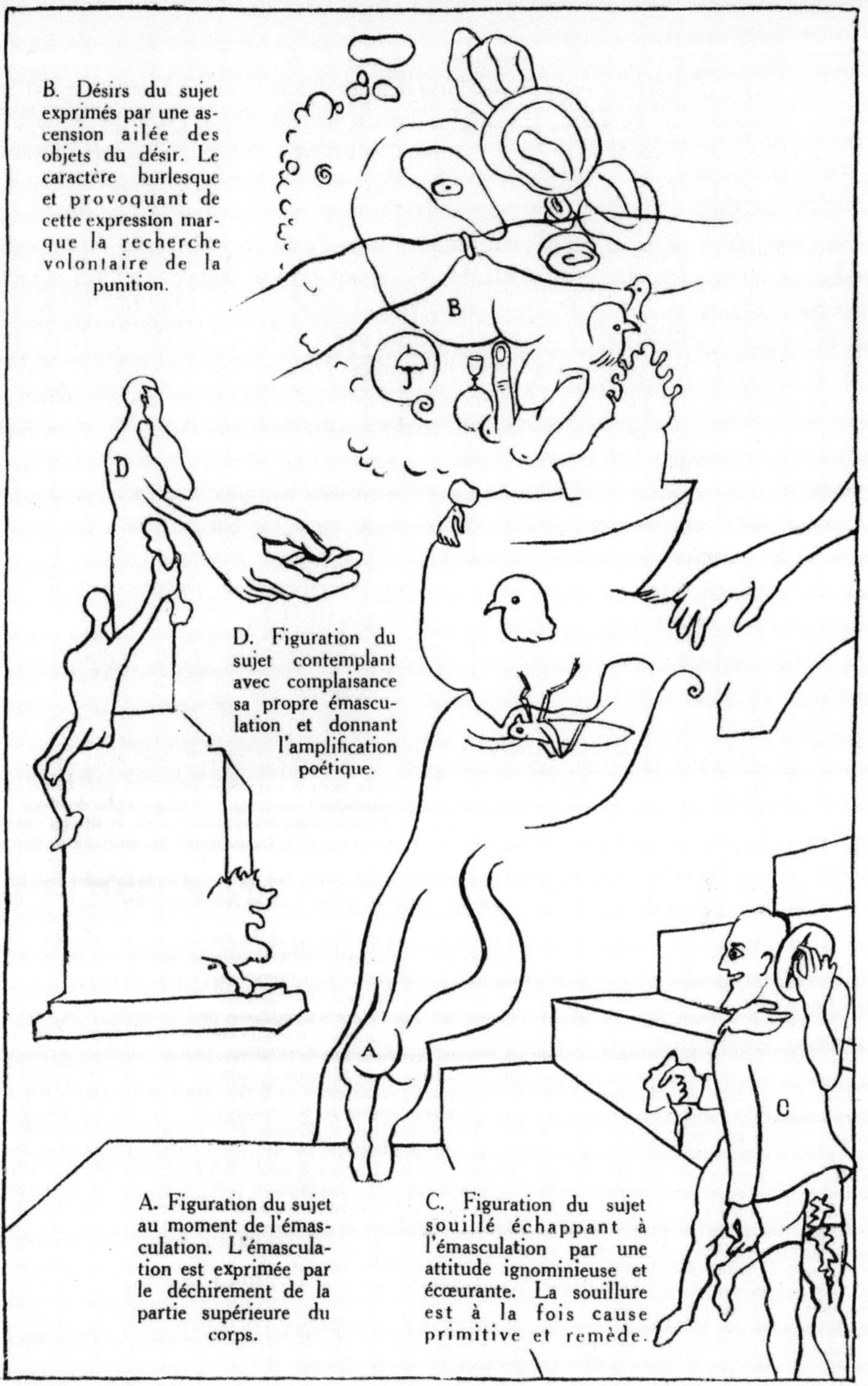

B. Désirs du sujet exprimés par une ascension ailée des objets du désir. Le caractère burlesque et provoquant de cette expression marque la recherche volontaire de la punition.
B
D
D. Figuration du sujet contemplant avec complaisance sa propre émasculation et donnant l'amplification poétique.
A
C
A. Figuration du sujet au moment de l'émasculation. L'émasculation est exprimée par le déchirement de la partie supérieure du corps.
C. Figuration du sujet souillé échappant à l'émasculation par une attitude ignominieuse et écœurante. La souillure est à la fois cause primitive et remède.

SCHÉMA PSYCHANALYTIQUE DES FIGURATIONS CONTRADICTOIRES DU SUJET DANS " LE JEU LUGUBRE " DE SALVADOR DALI.

listening to Pujols, who declared in the text cited above that the Sagrada Família was the bonfire on which burned all of the 'waste of architectural constructions of history' and called its steeples 'four tongues of fire more condensed than ice'.[110] How are we to avoid associating these steeples with those chimneys?

Gaudí's architecture, and by extension *modern style* architecture, was the quintessential *religious* architecture that emerges from childhood. Bataille wrote of factory chimneys that 'as a terrified child' he 'discerned in those giant scarecrows [...] the presence of a frightful rage' that would later become his own, 'giving meaning to everything spoiling within [his] own head and to all that which, in civilized states, looms up like carrion in a nightmare'.[111] Shortly after the publication of 'L'âne pourri', René Crevel claimed in his 1931 *Dalí ou l'anti-obscurantisme* that Gaudí's architecture emerges 'from the volcanoes of rage'.[112] What rage is this if not that of Bataille's terrified childhood, and what are those volcanoes but the cold fires of 'stone, wax and oil' evoked by Pujols?[113] In *modern style* architecture, Dalí writes in 'L'âne pourri', the 'most violent and cruel automatism pitifully betrays a hatred of reality and a need to seek refuge in an ideal world, just as occurs in infantile neurosis'.[114] Certainly in Bataille's texts on architecture—at least—Dalí found the arguments, expressions and places that *imposed order* on the figures through which he saw the 'deformed and monstrous' architecture of Art Nouveau or, simply, the *maniera* in which to excavate the bestial metaphors of Pujols—or, in short, the tools with which to 'systematize the confusion' of Pujols and *Modernisme* so as to create the paradigms of his own 'modern mythology': that of a new and estranged 'Paris peasant'.

Imposing order, without paradoxes: that is what Dalí did throughout 1928 in the scattered illustrations of *La Révolution surréaliste*, seeking with his painting to forge whatever links were possible between the images of Arp, Tanguy, Ernst, Masson and Miró that the magazine published here and there in its pages, without much commentary, and independently of the texts—essentially as *illustrations*—so that all those 'celibate machines' could finally marry—that *marier les amoureux* of Ozenfant, a model from which Dalí had not yet completely divorced himself—and live happily.

To see what I mean we need only glance at Arp's *Table, montagne, ancres et nombril*, on page 10 of No. 7 of *La Révolution surréaliste*; at Ernst's *La belle saison*, on page 7 of No. 8; at Miró's *Personnage jetant une pierre à un oiseau*, on page 62 of No. 9-10; at Tanguy's *Dessin*, on page 22 of the same issue, and a few more, such as Masson's automatic drawings and sand paintings, and compare them with Dalí's works of the same year, in the following order, for example: *Soleil, La vache spectrale, Baigneuse, L'oiseau blessé* .... In other words, if all these illustrations were published under the Bretonian title 'Surrealism and Painting' (the 'and' is ambiguously disjunctive),[115] Dalí had imposed on himself the task of bringing together all of the *disiecti membra poetae*—the expression was never more apt—in a 'surrealist painting' that was not short of scattered members.

The operation continued in 1929, but now through the manipulation of a somewhat different mass of material: on the one hand, a method—the paranoiac-critical method—that would gather in all of the *stories* of psychoanalysis and turn Dalí's paintings into stories — or novels, as Aragon waspishly remarked;[116] on the other, architectural elements that are quite plainly far from remote fossils, 'terrifying and edible'—but cooled; cold cuts—surfacing from a collective childhood that is always interpreted as neurosis, and is but the *demodée* hyperaesthesia of the decadents converted into hyperaesthetics.

In the pictures Dalí painted in the summer of 1929, some of which were shown at the end of the year in his first Paris exhibition at the Galerie Goemans, we find Art Nouveau elements and ornamental details everywhere, along with a whole series of obsessive tropes related to childhood.

The Great Masturbator [fig. 220], with its mouldings inspired by domestic *bibelots* and its Pre-Raphaelite figures, could be said to condense all of these images. But there is another work that seems to me from this point of view—and of course there are many others—to be even more important: *Monument impérial à la femme-enfant* [fig. 224], with its child-woman[117] and its rock formation incrusted with fossils; fossils of sea waves, of gigantic flowers, of long streaming hair, of bodies and busts in ecstasy, of butterflies petrified at the moment of taking wing, of the smoke of a a cigarette that seems to turn into a buttress of the whole rock, which has been mineralized just as it began to sprout heads of all kinds, ultimate forms of the sea foam or the whorls of smoke...

Everything that constitutes the mythology of Art Nouveau is present here, arrested in that eternity of yesterday of which we have already spoken, and accompanied now by the new system of guarantees underpinning Dalí's work: Napoleon (in other words, Meissonier), the *Monna Lisa,* Millet's *Angélus* ....

106 VERS UNE ARCHITECTURE

PAESTUM, de 600 à 550 av. J.-C.

Le Parthénon est un produit de sélection appliquée à un standart établi. Depuis un siècle déjà, le temple grec était organisé dans tous ses éléments.

Lorsqu'un standart est établi, le jeu de la concurrence immédiate et violente s'exerce. C'est le match; pour gagner, il faut

Cliché de *La Vie Automobile*. HUMBERT, 1907.

DES YEUX QUI NE VOIENT PAS... 107

Cliché Albert Morancé. PARTHÉNON, de 447 à 434 av. J.-C.

faire mieux que l'adversaire *dans toutes les parties*, dans la ligne d'ensemble et dans tous les détails. C'est alors l'étude poussée des parties. Progrès.

Le standart est une nécessité d'ordre apporté dans le travail humain.

Le standart s'établit sur des bases certaines, non pas arbi-

DELAGE, Grand-Sport 1921.

fig. 223

fig. 224

But where is this monolith standing? What do we see beneath it? On a pedestal or, more precisely, an altar whose classical design recalls those in some of the paintings of Perugino and Raphael, or their sarcophagi, we see a tiny masturbating man, Dalí himself, like a larva whose tail is stiffened in *modern style* mouldings and whose soft head wears a crown—and I will not speak now of this king of the house, this Infant Jesus—so that everything that happens in the picture seems to be the petrification of his dream.

A petrification of his dream, of course, is the kneeling skeleton, that still and eternally adoring image whose paradox we find in the rocking chair a little to the left, the most elementary and purely mechanical of the pieces of furniture endowed with somnambulistic life in this new and even more sinister *chambre double* of the paranoiac image; and a petrification of his dream is also the ruin that brings together on a single platform those broken classical columns and that mineralized, vegetized motor car turned into a spring, like a contraction of all the punishments of the *Metamorphoses*.

But didn't the most famous facing pages of *Vers une architecture* [fig. 223] confront two Greek temples with two modern motor cars?[118] Above, Le Corbusier placed photographs of the temple of Paestum, 600-550 BC, and the Parthenon, 447-434 BC, and below a 1907 Humbert Cabriolet and a 1921 Delage Grand Sport. Was Le Corbusier comparing the beauty of those classical temples with that of the modern cars? Yes, but not only that. In fact, there was something much more important: what was being compared was the transition from Paestum to the Parthenon and the transition from the Humbert to the Delage, that is to say, the time taken by the respective advances. Temples and automobiles are constructed on the basis of standards that cannot change, Le Corbusier is saying: only the productivity of perfection is what we see here, converted into stylization.

Vers une architecture concludes with a magnificent series of photographs of the Parthenon by Boissonnas, which is exalted above all for the perfection of its details, its machinist accuracy. In his speech at the meeting in Sitges Dalí had said it would be preferable if all that remained of the Parthenon were a good photo essay rather than its ruins, and in February 1929 he repeated this opinion in 'La dada fotogràfica'; by the summer of that same year the motor car is already a fossil in the middle of film-set ancient ruins. 'Immortal Ruins', haunted by the ghosts of the *modern style* in a *becoming* that, without paradox, is always deferred.

NOTES

'I PROPOSE TO MAKE A SERIOUS STUDY OF ORNAMENTATION'

1. The original manuscript is in the Museu Comarcal Salvador Vilaseca in Reus. Of the various transcripts, by far the best is: *Gaudí, Antoni. Escritos y documentos*, pp. 41 and ff. Mercader, Laura (ed.). Barcelona: El Acantilado, 2002.

2. Id., p. 69.

3. Id., p. 70.

4. Id., pp. 68-69. The following quotations are also from these two pages.

5. See Lahuerta, Juan José. *On Loos, Ornament and Crime. Columns of Smoke*, Vol. II. Barcelona: Tenov Books, 2015.

6. Gaudí, Antoni. Op. cit.,Id., pp. 135-148 and 165-175.

7. Id., pp. 50-52. The following quotations are also from these two pages.

8. The review was published in two instalments in *La Renaixensa*, Barcelona, on the 1st and 2nd of February 1881. Now in: Gaudí, Antoni. Op. cit., pp. 165-175.

9. Id., p. 167.

10. Id., p. 168.

11. Id., p. 171.

12. There is only a very short entry for 'Décoration': Viollet-le-Duc, Eugène. *Dictionnaire Raisonné de l'Architecture Française du XIe au XVIe siécle*, Vol. V, p. 26. Paris: Librairies Imprimeries Réunies, 1860. The subject of ornamentation is dispersed among other entries, such as 'Flore': see note 19.

13. Id., p. 41.

14. Id., pp. 54-55. The following quotations are also from these two pages.

15. See Lahuerta, Juan José. *Antoni Gaudí, 1852-1926, Architecture, Ideology and Politics*, pp. 47 and ff. Milan: Electa, (1993) 2003. See too, regarding his student projects, related to these notes: id., *Gaudí Universe*, pp. 15 and ff. Barcelona / Madrid: Centre de Cultura Contemporània de Barcelona, Museo Nacional Centro de Arte Reina Sofía, 2002.

16. Jones, Owen. *The Grammar of Ornament*. London: Day and Son Ltd., 1856. (with 100 colour lithographs). A second edition with 112 plates was published by Bernard Quaritch, London, 1868.

17. On the function of the void in Gaudí's work see Lahuerta, Juan José. *Gaudí Universe*, cit., pp. 78 and ff.

18. Gaudí, Antoni. Op. cit., p. 95.

19. Viollet-le-Duc, Eugène. 'Flore', op. cit., Vol. V, pp. 485-486.

20. Ruskin, John. *Our Fathers Have Told Us. Sketches of the History of Christendom for Boys and Girls Who Have Been Held at Its Fonts… Part I. The Bible of Amiens*. Sunnyside, Orpington, Kent: George Allen, 1884; Proust, Marcel. 'Préface', in: id., *La Bible d'Amiens*. Paris: Éditions du Mercure de France, 1904.
(I quote from the Spanish edition with introduction and notes by Calatrava, Juan: id., *La Biblia de Amiens*, pp. 77-78. Madrid: Abada Editores, 2006).

21. Gaudí, Antoni. Op. cit., p. 59.

22. Id.

23. Haeckel, Ernst. *Kunstformen der Natur*. Leipzig & Vienna: Bibliographisches Institut, 1904. See, too, for example, the plates in his much earlier *Die Radiolarien*. Berlin: Georg Reimer Verlag, 1862.

'LA PÂTISSERIE BARCELONE'

24. Picarol (Costa Ferrer, Josep), 'Sobre aixo del concurs de edificis y fatxadas', *L'Esquella de la Torratxa*, No. 1398, Barcelona, 20 October 1905, pp. 888.

25. Huysmans, Joris-Karl. *À rebours*. Paris: Charpentier, 1884. (I use the edition by M. Fumaroli: id., op. cit., Gallimard, Paris, 1996); Goncourt, Edmond de. *La maison d'un artiste*, 2 vols. Paris: Charpentier, 1881.

26. Loos, Adolf. 'Von einem armen, reichen Mann', *Neues Wiener Tagblatt*, Vienna, 26 April 1900.

27. Veblen, Thorstein. *The Theory of the Leisure Class*. New York: The Macmillan Company, 1899; Simmel, Georg. *Philosophie des*

Geldes, Duncker & Humblot. Leipzig: 1900; Sombart,Werner. *Luxus und Kapitalismus.* Munich & Leipzig: Duncker & Humblodt, 1913.

28. Flaubert, Gustave. *Le dictionnaire des idées reçues ou Le catalogue des opinions chic*, first published in: *Œuvres complètes de Gustave Flaubert. Bouvard et Pécuchet. Œuvre posthume*, p. 415. Paris: Louis Conard, 1910.

29. Santiago Rusiñol (1861-1931). Painter, writer, playwright and collector, he studied in Paris and was one of the key figures in Catalan Modernisme, organizing gatherings in the Barcelona tavern Els Quatre Gats and Modernista festivities at Cau Ferrat, his house-cum-studio in Sitges. From a wealthy family, he travelled widely and gave financial assistance to poorer artists such as Casas, Utrillo and Picasso. *Ed.*

30. Canals, Salvador. 'Los que son algo. Santiago Rusinol', *El diario del Teatro*, No. 20, Madrid, 14 January 1895, pp. 1-2; id., *La Vanguardia*, Barcelona, 18 January 1895, p. 1.

31. Brunet, Llorenç. 'Barcelona nueva', *El Diluvio. Suplemento ilustrado*, Barcelona, 27 January 1906, pp. 56-57.

32. *Papitu*, No. 20, Barcelona, 27 January 1909, p. 164.

33. Francesc Pujols (1882-1962). Autodidact and dilettante, author of poetry and plays, political and philosophical essays and art criticism, and a regular contributor to several newspapers, he was respected in intellectual circles even though his ironic and sometimes humorous manner was out of step with the *Noucentista* Catalan cultural establishment. Of note among his works are *Hiparxiología*, his thoughts on how to live the good life, and *La visió artística i religiosa d'en Gaudí*, his particular interpretation of Gaudí's work, subsequently championed by Dalí. *Ed.*

34. Pujols, Francesc. Untitled. *Picarol*, No. 6, Barcelona, March 1912, p. 11.

35. Puiggarí, Josep. *Monografía de la casa-palau i museu del Escm. Sr. D. Eusebi Güell y Bacigalupi*, p. 6. Barcelona: Centre Excursionista de Catalunya – Tipografía L'Avenç, 1894; Rahola, Frederic. 'Palacio de Güell in Barcelona. Planeado y construido por Gaudí', *La Vanguardia*, Barcelona, 3 August 1890, pp. 4-5.

36. *Papitu*, No. 45, Barcelona, 6 October 1909, p. 731. The so-called Casa Ballarín was an iron foundry specializing in artistic work, established in Barcelona in 1885 by Manuel Ballarín, who also made the streetlamps on Passeig de Gràcia designed by Pere Falqués, his brother-in-law. In 1900 Ballarín also began making safes, hence the pun in the cartoon caption: in Catalan *cases fortes*, 'strong houses', sounds very much like *caixes fortes*, meaning 'safes' or 'strong boxes'.

37. Caran d'Ache, 'Le cordon bleu. On peut se mettre à table!', *Le Figaro*, Paris, 9 April 1900, p. 3.

38. Dalí, Salvador. 'De la beauté terrifiante et comestible de l'architecture Modern'style', *Minotaure*, No. 3/4, Paris, December 1933, pp. 69-77. The manuscript is in the Centre for Dalinian Studies at the Fundació Gala-Salvador Dalí in Figueres. For a comparison with the published text see: Dalí, Salvador. *Obra Completa. Vol. IV, Ensayos I. Articles 1919-1986*, pp. 304-320. Edited by Lahuerta, Juan José. Barcelona: Destino, 2005.

39. Ruskin, John. Op. cit., p. 267.

40. Carco, Francis. *Printemps d'Espagne*, pp. 275-276. Paris: Albin Michel, 1929.

41. *Cu-Cut!*, Barcelona, 23 March 1910, p. 186.

42. *Cu-Cut!*, Barcelona, 1 February 1912, p. 76.

43. *Cu-Cut!*, Barcelona, 25 February 1909, n. p.

44. Josep Carner (1884-1970). Poet and journalist, he was one of the main creators of the aesthetic canon of Noucentisme, the Catalan cultural and political movement that reacted against Modernisme in favour of classicism. *Ed.*

45. Carner, Josep. 'L'auca del senyor Gaudí', in: *Auques i ventalls*. Barcelona: Marian Galve, 1914.

46. The type of spittoon seen in the photograph was designed by Juan Escudero in 1907 and patented in 1909.

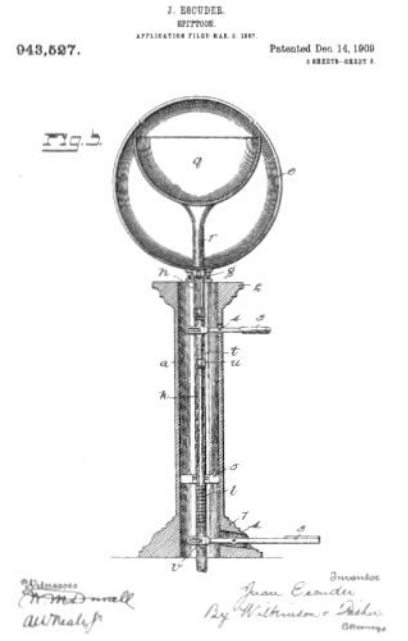

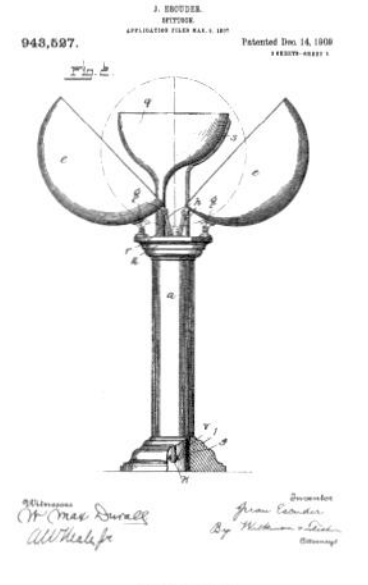

47. See note 23.

48. Baudelaire, Charles. 'La chambre double', *Le spleen de Paris*, 1869. (I quote from: id., *Œuvres complètes*, Vol. I, p. 280. Pichois, Claude ed. Paris: Gallimard, 1975).

49. See note 26.

50. See notes 44 and 45.

51. Baudelaire, Charles. *Les Paradis artificiels* (1860), in: id., *Œuvres complètes*, cit., p. 399; Huysmans, Joris-Karl. Op. cit., p. 187.

52. Corominas, 'Temps a venir', *Cu-Cut!*, Barcelona, 30 October 1902, p. 723.

53. Lombroso, Cesare. *L'uomo di genio*. Turin: Fratelli Bocca, 1888. (I use the French translation: id., *L'homme de génie*, p. 304. Paris: Alcan, 1889).

54. We consider this personage at length in: Lahuerta, Juan José. *On Loos, Ornament and Crime. Columns of Smoke*, Vol. II. Barcelona: Tenov Books, 2015.

55. Bückmann, Ingolf. 'Antoni Gaudí: ein pathographischer Versuch, zugleich ein Beitrag zur Genese des Genieruhms', *Zeitschrift für die Gesamte Neurologie und Psychiatric*, No. 139, 1932, pp. 133-157.

56. Pujols, Francesc. Op. cit., p. 11.

57. Català, Jordi. *L'arquitecte i el diable*. Col·lecció d'En Patufet. Barcelona: Boguñà, 1928.

FIRE AND ASHES

Behold the Work of Restoration of Capitalism

58. See notes 33 and 34.

59. Tragic Week: A grassroots antimilitarist and anticlerical revolt that took place between July 26 and August 2, 1909. The mobilizations of reservists for the war in Melilla were the trigger for a latent social conflict, as men from wealthy families could exempt themselves from serving in the Second Rif War by paying a sum far beyond the reach of the working classes. A general strike on July 26, 1909 paralyzed the industrial towns and cities of Catalonia and led to armed clashes in Barcelona, resulting in the burning of many religious buildings. The unrest was harshly repressed by the army and armed police; a state of emergency was decreed, newspapers, workers' cultural centres and secular schools were closed and summary detentions and military trials ended with five civilians executed, in the face of international protests. *Ed.*

60. See notes 44 and 68.

61. Pujols, Francesc. *La visió artística i religiosa d'en Gaudí*, p. 29. Barcelona: Llibreria Catalònia, 1927.

62. Id., p. 29.

63. Joan Maragall (1860-1911). Poet and writer, a key figure in the revival of Catalan culture in the nineteenth century and a leading member of *La Renaixença*, he was one of the most admired and influential intellectuals in turn-of-the-century Barcelona, both as an innovator in literature and aesthetics and for his vision modern and cosmopolitan politics. *Ed.*

64. The articles on the Sagrada Família are: Maragall, Joan. 'El templo que nace' (The temple that is born), *Diario de Barcelona*, Barcelona, 20 December 1900; id., 'Una gràcia de caritat...!' (A grace of charity), *Diario de Barcelona*, 7 November 1905; id., 'En la Sagrada Família' (In the Sagrada Família), *Diario de Barcelona*, 19 March 1906; id., 'Fuera del tiempo' (Out of time), *Forma*, No. 16, Barcelona, 1907, now in: id., *Obres completes*,

Vol. II, pp. 614, 705, 726 and 768, respectively. Barcelona: Selecta, 1981. Also reprinted in: Lahuerta, Juan José (ed.). *Antoni Gaudí (1852-1926). Antología contemporánea*, pp. 41-52. Madrid: Alianza Editorial, 2002.

65. Caldes d'Estrac, a small town thirty miles up the coast from Barcelona where many well-to-do families had a summer residence. *Ed.*

66. Letter to Torras i Bages, 11 September 1909, in: Maragall, Joan. *Obres Completes*, Vol. I, p. 1157. Barcelona: Selecta, 1981.

67. Maragall, Joan. 'Ah! Barcelona...', *La Veu de Catalunya*, Barcelona, 1 October 1909; id., 'La iglésia cremada', *La Veu de Catalunya*, Barcelona, 18 December, 1909, and 'La ciutat del perdó', dated 10 October 1909. These three articles are now in: id., *Obres Completes*, Vol. I, cit., pp. 775-782. Subsequent quotations are also from this source.

68. Josep Torras i Bages (1846-1916). Bishop of Vic and Barcelona, a writer and founder of conservative Catholic Catalan nationalism. Among his many other occupations, he gave weekly lectures in the Cercle Artístic Sant Lluc, frequented by Antoni Gaudí. *Ed.*

69. Enric Prat de la Riba (1870-1917). Conservative Catalan intellectual and politician who was president of the council of Barcelona from 1907 and of the Mancomunitat or Commonwealth of Catalonia from 1914 until his untimely death in 1917. He published articles on culture and politics as well as on economic and legal issues. *Ed.*

70. Eugeni d'Ors (1881-1951). Writer who coined the term Noucentisme, he disseminated his idea of an urban, cosmopolitan, conservative and elitist culture through his columns in the newspaper *La Veu de Catalunya* from 1906. Between 1911 and 1920 he was director of the Institute of Catalan Studies, from where he established Noucentisme as the leading cultural programme of the period. *Ed.*

71. Benet, Josep. *Maragall davant la Setmana Trágica.* Barcelona: Edicions 62, 1964 (2nd ed.), is still essential reading on this subject.

72. Friedrich, Ernst. *Krieg dem kriege!*, Vol. I., p. 183. Berlin: Internationale Kriegsmuseum, 1930.

73. See G. Romero, Pedro. *F.X. Sobre la fi de l'art. La Setmana Tràgica.* Generalitat de Catalunya. Barcelona: Departament de Cultura, 2002.

74. Edmund Burke's *A Philosophical Enquiry into the Origin of Our Ideas of the Sublime and Beautiful.* London: R. & J. Dodsley, 1757. On the sublime and ruins, see the excellent González García, Ángel. *Arte y terror.* Barcelona: Mudito & Co., 2008.

75. Barbey d'Aurevilly, Jules. *L'ensorcelée* Paris: Librairie Nouvelle, 1858. Published in instalments in 1852 and in book form for the first time in 1854; Huysmans, Joris-Karl. *La cathédrale.* Paris: Stock, 1898.

76. See Lahuerta, Juan José. *On Loos, Ornament and Crime. Columns of Smoke*, Vol. II. Barcelona: Tenov Books, 2015.

77. Nordau, Max. *Entartung.* Berlin: Duncker, 1892. (I quote from id., *Dégénérescence*, Vol. I, p. 132. Paris: Alcan, 1984).

78. Riera, Augusto. *Semana Trágica. Relato de la sedición e incendios in Barcelona and Cataluña.* Barcelona: Barcino Editorial Hispano-Americana,1909.

79. *La semana sangrienta (Sucesos de Barcelona).* Barcelona: Editorial Ibero-Americana: 1909.

80. Brissa, José. *La Revolución de Julio en Barcelona. Su represión. Sus víctimas. Proceso de Ferrer.* Barcelona: Editorial Maucci, 1910.

81. Francesc Ferrer i Guàrdia (1859-1909). Educator and thinker with progressive republican views who gradually turned to anarchism, he came into contact with the principles of secular and libertarian education in Paris. In 1901 he founded the Escuela Moderna in Barcelona, a modern school for the middle-class children, independent of State and Church and based on rationalism. Though innocent, he was sentenced to death as the instigator of the Tragic Week and executed on October 13, 1909; subsequently, the international campaign against his wrongful conviction brought down the government. *Ed.*

82. *La Actualidad*, special compilation issue, Barcelona, 28 August 1909. The same magazine had devoted a number of previous covers to the same subject. For example: id., No. 158, Barcelona, 10 August 1909.

83. Bas, Martí. *L'Esquella de la Torratxa*, Barcelona, 23 july 1937.

The Temptation of Man

84. See, for example: Lombroso, Cesare. *L'uomo delinquent.* Turin: Bocca, 1878 (I use the 1897 edition); Lombroso, Cesare; Ferrero, Guglielmo. *La donna delinquente. La prostituta e la donna normale.* Turin: Roux, 1894; Bertillon, Alphonse. *Identification anthropometrique. Instructions signaletiques.* Melun: Imprimerie Administrative, 1893.

85. See note 29.

86. Lombroso, Cesare. Ferrero; Guglielmo. Op. cit. I quote here and elsewhere from the French edition, *La femme criminale et la prostituée*, p. 319. Paris: Alcan, 1896.

87. On 7 November 1893 the anarchist Santiago Salvador threw two bombs into the stalls of the Gran Teatre del Liceu, killing twenty people in the audience, in an individual action of protest at the execution of the anarchist Paulí Pallàs, who had tried to assassinate the military governor of Catalonia. Salvador escaped, but was arrested two months later and executed in November 1894. At the end of the 19th c. The Liceu opera house was a favourite rendezvous of the Catalan bourgeoisie, and a clear symbol of the ruling oligarchy. The attack caused great commotion in the city; the theatre remained closed for several months and the seats in the area where the bomb exploded were left unoccupied for several years.

88. Maragall, Joan. 'Paternal', in: *Obres Completes*, Vol. I, cit., p. 90.

89. Crevel, René. *Dalí ou l'anti-obscurantisme.* Paris: Éditions Surréalistes, 1931.

90. Pouzyna, Ivan. *Lénine 'le Grand'*, pp. 87-88. Paris: Nouvelles Éditions Latines, 1950.

'Immortal Ruins'

91. Now in Breton, André. *Œuvres complètes*, Vol. I, p. 1027. París: Gallimard, 1988. Bonnet, Marguerite (ed.); Dalí, Salvador. *La femme visible.* Paris: Éditions Surréalistes, 1930.

92. Ozenfant, Amedée; Jeanneret, Charles-Édouard. 'Sur la plastique', *L'Esprit Nouveau*, No. 1, Paris, October 1920, p. 45.

93. Verne, Henri; Chavance, René. *Pour comprendre l'art décoratif en France*, p. 10. Paris: Hachette, 1925.

94. Le Corbusier, 'Où en est l'architecture?', *L'Architecture Vivante*, Paris, Autumn-Winter 1927, pp. 7-11.

95. Zervos, Christian. 'Gaudí. Editorial Canosa. Barcelone', *Cahiers d'Art*, IV, Paris, 1929, suppl. p. XVII.

96. Morand, Paul. *1900.* Paris: Les Éditions de France, 1931.

97. Myself [C. Soldevila]. *L'art d'ensenyar Barcelona. Manual del cicerone amateur que vol quedar bé, tot fent quedar bé la ciutat.* Barcelona: Llibreria Catalònia, 1929.

98. Morand, Paul. 'La nuit catalane', in: *Ouvert la nuit*, pp. 13 and ff. Paris: Éditions de la Nouvelle Revue Française, 1922; Carco, Francis. Op. cit., pp. 247 and ff.

99. Folch i Torres, Joaquim. 'L'ordre', *La Veu de Catalunya*, Barcelona, 7 April 1910.

100. See note 61.

101. Bataille, Georges. 'Architecture', *Documents*, No. 2, Paris, May 1929, p. 117.

102. Id., 'Abattoir', 'Cheminée d'usine', *Documents*, No. 6, Paris, November 1929, pp. 328-332.

103. Id., 'Friandise cannibale', *Documents*, No. 4, Paris, September 1929, p. 216.

104. Id., 'Le jeu lugubre', *Documents*, No. 7, Paris, December 1929, pp. 369-372.

105. Dalí, Salvador. 'L'âne pourri', *Le Surréalisme au Service de la Révolution*, No. 1, Paris, July 1930, pp. 9-12.

106. Dalí, Salvador. 'La fotografia, pura creació de l'esperit', *L'Amic de les Arts*, II, No. 18, Sitges, 30 September 1927, pp. 90-91; id., 'Per a el "meeting" de Sitges. Els 7 devant "El Centaure"', *L'Amic de *les Arts*, No. 25, Sitges, 31 May 1928, pp. 194-195; id., 'La dada fotográfica', *Gaseta de les Arts*, second epoch, No. 6, Barcelona, February 1929, pp. 40-42.

107. Le Corbusier. *Vers une architecture*, p. 243. Paris: G. Crès et Cie., 1924 (2nd ed.).

108. See note 38.

109. Id., 'L'âne pourri', cit.

110. Pujols, Francesc. Op. cit., pp. 29 and 35.

111. Bataille, Georges. 'Cheminée d'usine', op. cit., pp. 329 and 332.

112. Crevel, René. Op. cit., p. 27.

113. Pujols, Francesc. Op. cit., p. 26.

114. Dalí, Salvador. 'L'âne pourri', cit., p. 12.

115. The first drafts of 'Le Surréalisme et la peinture' appeared in successive issues of *La Révolution surréaliste* between 1925 and 1927. It was published in book form by Éditions de la Nouvelle Revue Française, Librarie Gallimard, Paris, 1928, and in further expanded form by Brentano, New York, 1945.

116. Aragon, Louis. *La peinture au défi*, Galerie Goemans, Paris, 1930, p. 27.

117. For more on the child-woman see: Lahuerta, Juan José. *On Loos, Ornament and Crime. Columns of Smoke*, Vol. II. Barcelona: Tenov Books, 2015.

118. Le Corbusier. Op. cit., pp. 106-107.

LIST OF ILLUSTRATIONS

'I PROPOSE TO MAKE A SERIOUS STUDY OF ORNAMENTATION'

1. Durandelle, Louis-Émile. 'Construction of the Church of Sacré-Cœur in Montmartre',1882.

2. The Sacré-Cœur Basilica in Montmartre in construction. Postcard, c. 1905.

3. Durandelle, Louis-Émile. 'View from the Interior and Iron Framework of the Hall'; 'Construction of the Paris Opéra'. 1867. © Victoria and Albert Museum, London.

4. Durandelle, Louis-Émile. 'Work of Construction of the Sacré-Cœur'. 1877-1882.

5. Durandelle, Louis-Émile. 'View of the East Façade', 1867. © Victoria and Albert Museum, London.

6. L'Ópéra de Paris. Postcard, c. 1906.

7. Durandelle, Louis-Émile. 'Projecting tables. Side galleries of the Grand Staircase'. Id. *Le Nouvel Opéra de Paris: Statues décoratives, groupes et bas-reliefs* [The New Paris Opéra: Decorative statues, groups and bas-reliefs]. Paris: Ducher, 1875. © Biblioteca Nacional de España, Madrid.

8. Garnier, Charles. 'Detail of the main façade'. *Le Nouvel Opéra de Paris* [The New Paris Opéra]. Paris: Ducher, 1876. Courtesy of the Col·legi d'Arquitectes de Catalunya. Photo: Suñé, Alba.

9. Durandelle, Louis-Émile. 'Masks in the Control vestibule', 1867. Courtesy of the Getty's Open Content Program.

10. Garnier, Charles. 'Detail of the main façade: Grand proscenium tympanum'. *Le Nouvel Opéra de Paris* [The New Paris Opéra]. Paris: Ducher, 1876.
Courtesy of the Col·legi d'Arquitectes de Catalunya. Photo: Suñé, Alba.

11. Durandelle, Louis-Émile. 'Pegasus'. 1867.

12-14. Jones, Owen. *The Grammar of Ornament,* 1856. Plates XLII, XL and XXXLII. London: Bernard Quarritch, 1868. Courtesy of the Col·legi d'Arquitectes de Catalunya. Photo: Suñé, Alba.

15. Gaudí, Antoni. Smoking room of the Vicens house, 1905. © Fundació Institut Amatller d'Art Hispànic. Arxiu Mas.

16. Jones, Owen. Id. Plate XXXLL.

17. Stables of the Güell estate in Pedralbes, Barcelona, c. 1890. Courtesy of the Càtedra Gaudí. © Càtedra Gaudí-ETSAB-UPC.

18. Detail of the façade of the stables of the Güell estate. Photo: J.T.

19-20. De Morgan, William. Designs for single and two-piece tiles, c. 1872 and 1898. © Victoria and Albert Museum, London.

21. Gaudí, Antoni. El Capricho estate in Comillas, Santander, 1883-1885. Postcard, c. 1920.

22. Id. Photo: © Pere Vivas / Triangle Postals.

23. Id. Detail of the tiles at El Capricho. Photo: © Pere Vivas / Triangle Postals.

24. Gaudí, Antoni. Vicens house in Sant Gervasi, Barcelona, 1883-1885. 'Barcelona, modern constructions. Calle de S. Gervasio, núm. 24.' Postcard, Barcelona: A.T.V., c. 1910.

25. Id. Detail of the façade. Photo: © Pere Vivas / Triangle Postals.

26. Id. Detail of the tiles. Photo: © Pere Vivas / Triangle Postals.

27-29. Id. Gate of the Vicens house, general view and details from the outside and inside. Photos: © Pere Vivas / Triangle Postals.

30. Id. Dragon on the gate of the Güell estate in Pedralbes, c. 1950. Courtesy of the Càtedra Gaudí. © Càtedra Gaudí-ETSAB-UPC.

31. Id. The gate from the inside, c. 1950. Courtesy of the Càtedra Gaudí. © Càtedra Gaudí-ETSAB-UPC.

32-35. Id. Details. Photo: J.T.

36. Id. Dining room of the Vicens house. Photo: © Pere Vivas / Triangle Postals.

37. Id. The gallery with fountain of the Vicens house, c. 1890.

38. Id. Papier-mâché bird from the Vicens house. Photo: © Pere Vivas / Triangle Postals

39. Güell estate. General view from the exterior, c. 1890. Courtesy of the Càtedra Gaudí. © Càtedra Gaudí-ETSAB-UPC.

40. Id. The dragon on the gate, c. 1890. Courtesy of Càtedra Gaudí. © Càtedra Gaudí-ETSAB-UPC.

41. Id. General view from the inside, c. 1890. Courtesy of the Càtedra Gaudí. © Càtedra Gaudí-ETSAB-UPC.

42. Id. The gate open, c. 1905. Courtesy of the Càtedra Gaudí. © Càtedra Gaudí-ETSAB-UPC.

43. 'Gate of the country estate of D. Eusebio Güell'. Postcard, Barcelona: A.T.V., c. 1910.

44. Viollet-le-Duc, Eugène Emmanuel. 'Flore', 'Fleureon' and 'Fleurus'. *Dictionnaire raisonné de l'architecture française du* XIe *au* XVIe *siècle.* Paris: Bance-Morel, 1858-1868. Courtesy of the Col·legi d'Arquitectes de Catalunya. Photo: Suñé, Alba.

45. Jones, Owen. Op. cit. Plate XCIX.

46. 'Solemn and beautiful celebration at the Colonia Güell'. *La Hormiga de Oro*, Barcelona,13 November 1915. Courtesy of the Càtedra Gaudí. © Càtedra Gaudí-ETSAB-UPC.

47. Gaudí, Antoni. Crypt of the Colonia Güell, Sta. Coloma de Cervelló, Barcelona, 1908-1914. Photo: J.T.

48. Id. Details of reused materials. Photo: J.T.

49. Id. Industrial needles reused as part of a gate. Photo: © Pere Vivas / Triangle Postals.

50. Id., detail. Photo: © Pere Vivas / Triangle Postals.

51. Id. Construction of the Crypt of the Colonia Güell, c. 1911. Courtesy of the Càtedra Gaudí. © Càtedra Gaudí-ETSAB-UPC.

52. The plaster workshop at the Sagrada Familia. Photo: Ferran, 1926. Courtesy of the Càtedra Gaudí. © Càtedra Gaudí-ETSAB-UPC.

53. The sculpture workshop at the Sagrada Familia, c. 1926. Courtesy of the Càtedra Gaudí. © Càtedra Gaudí-ETSAB-UPC.

54. Gaudí, Antoni. Detail of the Nativity façade of the Sagrada Familia. Anonymous stereoscopic photograph, c. 1908.

55. 'Photos of poultry used to model the friezes of the Nativity façade', c. 1908.

56. Puig i Cadafalch, Josep. Design for a hydraulic cement tile. *Mosaicos Escofet Tejera y Co.* Barcelona: Escofet, 1900. Courtesy of Escofet.

57-58. Domènech i Montaner, Lluís. Designs for hydraulic cement tiles. *Mosaicos Escofet Tejera y Co.* Barcelona: Escofet, 1900. Courtesy of Escofet.

59. Mould elements for the production of Gaudí's hydraulic cement tile. Courtesy of Escofet.

60. Gaudí, Antoni. Drawing for the hydraulic cement tile for the Batlló house, c. 1905.

61. Id., A hydraulic cement tile, c. 1908. Courtesy of Escofet.

62. Haeckel, Ernst. Plate 38. *Kunstformen der Natur.* Leipzig and Vienna: Verlag des Bibliographisches Institut, 1904.

63. Gaudí, Antoni. Hydraulic cement tile for the Batlló house, finally used in the Milà house. © Pere Vivas / Triangle Postals.

64. Haeckel, Ernst. Op. cit., plate 26.

'LA PÂTISSERIE BARCELONE'

65. Picarol. 'Sobre aixo del concurs de edificis y fatxadas' (About that competition for buildings and façades). *L'Esquella de la Torratxa.* Barcelona, 13 October 1906.

66. 'Paseo de Gracia. A group of modern constructions'. Postcard, Barcelona: J. Venini, c. 1910.

67. Puig i Cadafalch, Josep. Casa Amatller, 1898-1900. On the right is the original façade of the building that Gaudí remodelled in 1904. Photo from 1902.

68. Id. 'Barcelona, modern constructions. Paseo de Gracia No. 41'. Postcard, Barcelona: A.T.V., c. 1910.

69. Gaudí, Antoni. Casa Batlló 1904-1906. 'Barcelona, modern constructions. Paseo de Gracia No. 43'. Postcard, Barcelona: A.T.V., c. 1910.

70. 'Barcelona, modern constructions. Paseo de Gracia No. 43'. Postcard, Barcelona: A.T.V., c. 1911.

71. 'Barcelona, palatial modern houses. Paseo de Gracia No. 43. The Batlló house'. Postcard, c. 1910.

72. 'Paseo de Gracia, architect Gaudí'. Barcelona: B.Y.P., c.1910.

73. Lochard, Fernand. 'Le Grenier'. Edmond de Goncourt's house at Auteuil, May-June 1886. Bibliothèque nationale de France.

74. Madrazo, Ricardo de. *Marià Fortuny's Studio in Rome*, 1874. Fortuny's studio was the model of the artist's house for Eusebi Güell and Antoni Gaudí's generation. © Museu Nacional d'Art de Catalunya, Barcelona.

75. Gaudí, Antoni. Interior of the Palau Güell. c. 1910. © Fundació Institut Amatller d'Art Hispànic. Arxiu Mas.

76-77. 'Monumental Gate' and 'Palace of Illusions'. *Le Panorama de l'Exposition Universelle.* Paris: Librairie d'Art Ludovic Baschet, 1900.

78. Domènech i Montaner, Lluís. Lleó Morera house, 1904-1905. 'First Prize: Casa No. 35 on Paseo de Gracia, designed and supervised by the architect Mr Domenech y Muntaner.' *La Hormiga de Oro*, Barcelona, 30 June 1906.

79. Id. Domènech i Montaner, Lluís; Arnau, Eusebi (sculptor). Ground floor of the Lleó Morera house, occupied by the Audouard photography studio. Photo from 1906.

80. Gaudí, Antoni. Ground floor of the Batlló house, occupied by the Pathé Frères company. Photo from 1910. © Fundació Institut Amatller d'Art Hispànic. Arxiu Mas.

81. Picarol. 'Future Barcelona. The true fate of the Milà house'. *L'Esquella de la Torratxa*, Barcelona, 4 January 1912.

82. Smith, Ismael. 'The sudden squall of the other day', *Cu-Cut!*, Barcelona, 1 July 1909.

83. 'Barcelona - Paseo de Gracia'. Postcard, c. 1910.

84-85. Junceda, Joan García. *Cu-Cut!*, Barcelona, 3 January 1907.

86. Ros. 'The end of our monuments'. *L'Esquella de la Torratxa* Barcelona, 4 January 1912.

87. Falqués, Pere; Querol, Agustí. Monument to F. Soler (Pitarra), 1906. Postcard, 1909.

88. Brunet, Llorenç. 'New Barcelona'. *El Diluvio*, Barcelona, 27 January 1906.

89. Gaudí, Antoni. Park Güell, 1900-1914. View of the entrance pavilions in construction from the exterior. Photo: Iranzo, c. 1905. Courtesy of the Càtedra Gaudí. © Càtedra Gaudí-ETSAB-UPC.

90. Id., View of the entrance pavilions before work started on construction of the hypostyle hall, c. 1905.

91. Id., View of the entrance pavilions, c. 1906.

92-93. Id., Stereoscopic photographs of the entrance pavilions in construction, c. 1905.

94. Top floor and crown of the Batlló and Ametller façades. © Pere Vivas / Triangle Postals.

95. Apa (Elías, Feliu). Cartoon. *Papitu*, Barcelona, 27 January 1909.

96. Aragay, Josep. 'Blazing Barcelona'. *Picarol*, Barcelona, March 1912.

97. Aragay, Josep. 'Palace of Catalan architecture by Gr. A. M. Sr. Gaudí'. *Papitu*, August 1911.

98. Gaudí, Antoni. The Batlló house, Sketch of the new façade over the elevation of the existing building. Courtesy of the Càtedra Gaudí. © Càtedra Gaudí-ETSAB-UPC.

99. Id. The Batlló house in construction, c. 1906. Courtesy of the Col·legi d'Arquitectes de Catalunya.

100. Id. The Calvet house, 1898-1900. Postcard, c.1910.

101-102. Id. Palau Güell, 1886-1888. Postcard, Barcelona:
A.T.V. c. 1910.

103. Brunet, Llorenç. 'Model of mediaeval architecture, between a nest and a tomb, which strikes me as not bad'. *El Diluvio*. 5 March 1910.

104. Brunet, Llorenç. 'Grand exposition and sale of codfish guts'. *El Diluvio*, Barcelona, 25 February 1911.

105. Apa (Elias, Feliu). 'Cases fortes' (Strong-room houses). *Papitu*, Barcelona, 6 October 1909.

106. The Milà house in construction, 1909. Courtesy of the Càtedra Gaudí.
© Càtedra Gaudí-ETSAB-UPC.

107. Dalí, Salvador. 'De la beauté terrifiante et comestible de l'architecture Modern' Style'. *Minotaure* No. 3-4, December 1933.

108. Gaudí, Antoni. The Milà house,1906-1910.
'Modern constructions. Paseo de Gracia No. 91'.
Postcard, Barcelona: A.T.V., c. 1910.

109. Id. Photo c. 1910.

110. Junceda, Joan García. Cartoon. *Cu-Cut!* Barcelona, 23 March 1910.

111. Gaudí, Antoni. The Milà house. Stereoscopic photograph, c. 1911.

112. 'Barcelona - Paseo de Gracia'. Postcard. c. 1911.

113. Gaudí, Antoni. Roof of the Milà house, c. 1910. Fondo Josep Bayó. Courtesy of the Càtedra Gaudí. © Càtedra Gaudí-ETSAB-UPC.

114. Id. Roof of the Milà house, c. 1910. © Arxiu Fotogràfic Centre Excursionista de Catalunya.

115. Id. Milà house. Stereoscopic photograph, c. 1910.

116. Id. Batlló house.'House for rent on Paseo de Gracia'. *Arquitectura y Construcción*. Barcelona, October 1907.

117. Cornet i Palau, Gaietà. Cartoon. *Cu-Cut!*, Barcelona, 1 February 1912.

118. The block of discord. Stereoscopic photograph, c. 1925.

119. Caran d'Ache (Poiré, Emmanuel). 'Le Cordon Bleu'. Le Figaro, Paris, 9 April 1900.

120. 'Barcelona–Paseo de Gracia'. Postcard. A.T.V., c. 1910.121.

121. Opisso, Ricard. Cartoon. *Cu-Cut!* Barcelona, 25 February 1909. © VEGAP, Barcelona, 2016.

122. Paseo de Gracia in front of the 'block of discord'. Photo postcard, 1908.

123. Gaudí, Antoni. The Batlló house, entrance hall, 1927.
© Fundació Institut Amatller d'Art Hispànic. Arxiu Mas.

124. Id. The Batlló house, hall of the main apartment, 1927.
© Fundació Institut Amatller d'Art Hispànic. Arxiu Mas.

125. Id. The Batlló house, handrail of the main staircase. Photo: Glòria Falcón.

126. Id. The Batlló house, corridor, 1927.
© Fundació Institut Amatller d'Art Hispànic. Arxiu Mas.

127. Id. Park Güell. Stereoscopic photograph of, c. 1919.

128. Riou, Édouard. 'L'aquarium d'eau douce dans le jardin réservé' (The freshwater aquarium in the reserved garden). *Grand album de l'Exposition Universelle 1867*. Paris: Michel Lévy Frères, 1868.

129. Gaudí, Antoni .The Batlló house, fireplace.

130. Riou, Édouard. Illustration for: Verne, Jules. *Voyage au centre de la terre*, Paris: Hetzel, 1864.

131. Gaudí, Antoni. The Batlló house, chapel with the sculpture of the Holy Family by Josep Llimona, frame by Antoni Gaudí, candlesticks by Josep Maria Jujol, tabernacle by Joan Rubio i Bellver and Christ crucified by Carles Mani, 1927.
© Fundació Institut Amatller d'Art Hispànic. Arxiu Mas.

132. Id. The Batlló house, dining room, 1927. © Fundació Institut Amatller d'Art Hispànic. Arxiu Mas.

133. Id. The Batlló house, the dining room door, 1927. © Fundació Institut Amatller d'Art Hispànic. Arxiu Mas.

134. Gaudí, Antoni. The Batlló house, main drawing room, 1927. © Fundació Institut Amatller d'Art Hispànic. Arxiu Mas.

135. Id. Ceiling of the main drawing room, c. 1950.

136-137. Id. Light well. © Pere Vivas / Casa Batlló.

138. Id. Main drawing room. © Pere Vivas / Casa Batlló.

139. Neuville, Alphonse de. Illustration for: Verne, Jules. *Vingt mille lieues sous les mers*. Paris: Hetzel, 1869.

140. Gaudí, Antoni. The Batlló house, detail of the main drawing room. © Pere Vivas / Casa Batlló.

141. Id. Dining room. © Fundació Institut Amatller d'Art Hispànic. Arxiu Mas.

142. Id. Chair from the Batlló house, c. 1906. © Museu Nacional d'Art de Catalunya, Barcelona.

143. Id. Interior of a bedroom in the Palau Güell with the dressing table designed by Gaudí, c. 1888. Photo c. 1920.

144. Id. Dressing table designed for Isabel López de Güell, c. 1888.

145. Id. Furniture from the Batlló house, c. 1906. © Museu Nacional d'Art de Catalunya, Barcelona.

146. Id. Railing of the main door. Advertising leaflet of the builder Badia Miarnau, c. 1910.

147. Mira, Leroy. 'Maison Batlló'. *Materiaux et documents d'art espagnol* [Materials and documents of Spanish art]. Barcelona: Librería Parera, 1901-1916.

148. Gaudí, Antoni. The Batlló house, façade. © Pere Vivas / Triangle Postals.

149. Id. The Batlló house, detail of the balconies. © Pere Vivas / Triangle Postals.

150. Workshop of the Sagrada Família, with a prototype of the balconies of the Batlló house. c. 1920. Courtesy of the Càtedra Gaudí. © Càtedra Gaudí-ETSAB-UPC.

151. Corominas, 'The coming times'. *Cu-Cut!* Barcelona, 30 October 1902.

152. Picasso, Pablo. *Two Figures and a Cat*, 1902/3. MPB 50.492. © Sucesión Pablo Picasso, VEGAP, Madrid, 2016.

153. Picasso, Pablo. *Prone Nude*, 1902/3. MPB 110.534. © Sucesión Pablo Picasso, VEGAP, Madrid, 2016.

154. Gaudí, Antoni. The Batlló house, door of apartament G. © Pere Vivas / Casa Batlló.

155. Id. The Batlló house, lower end of a typical staircase railing. © Pere Vivas / Casa Batlló.

156. Id. The Batlló house, end of the staircase in front of apartament G. © Pere Vivas / Casa Batlló.

157. Mallol, Lluís. Cover for *L'arquitecte i el diable*, Barcelona, 1928.

158. Gaudí's workshop on the site of the Temple of the Sagrada Família, photographs by Ferran, 1926. Courtesy of the Col·legi d'Arquitectes de Catalunya.

FIRE AND ASHES

Behold the Work of Restoration of Capitalism

159-160. Columns of smoke rising from burning religious buildings during the Tragic Week in Barcelona, July 1909. Double page of *La Actualidad*, 28 August 1909, and postcard.

161. Gaudí, Antoni. Temple of the Sagrada Família, Barcelona, 1883-1926. Photograph, c. 1924.

162-183. *Sucesos de Barcelona* [Events of Barcelona]. A sample of the collection of 100 postcards de the Tragic Week. Barcelona: A.T.V., 1909.

184. Riera, Augusto. *La Semana Trágica. Relato de la sedición e incendios en Barcelona y*

Cataluña [The Tragic Week. Account of the sedition and fires in Barcelona and Catalonia]. Barcelona: Barcino, 1909.

185. *La semana sangrienta (Sucesos de Barcelona)* [The Bloody Week. Events of Barcelona]. Barcelona: Ibero-Americana, 1909.

186. Brissa, José. *La Revolución de Julio en Barcelona. Su represión. Sus víctimas. Proceso de Ferrer.* [The July Revolution in Barcelona. Its repression. Its victims. Trial of Ferrer]. Barcelona: Maucci, 1910.

187. *La Actualidad*, Barcelona, 10 August 1909, cover.

188. *La Actualidad*, Barcelona, 28 August 1909, cover.

189-191. Id., inside pages.

192. J.V., 'Conventos incendiados–Geronimas'.[Burned convents–Hieronymites] Postcard, 1909.

193. Bas, Martí. *L'Esquella de la Torratxa, Barcelona*, 23 July 1937.

194. *Sucesos de Barcelona.* Postcard No. 40 with the Sagrada Família in the background. Barcelona: A.T.V., 1909.

195. Gaudí, Antoni. Temple of the Sagrada Família in 1883. Fondo Dalmases. Courtesy of the Càtedra Gaudí. © Càtedra Gaudí-ETSAB-UPC.

196. Temple of the Sagrada Família, postcards. c. 1910-1930.

The Temptation of Man

197-198. Mir, Joaquim. *The Cathedral of the Poor.* Painting and preparatory drawing, 1898. © Museu Nacional d'Art de Catalunya, Barcelona.

199. Photograph taken during construction of the Sagrada Família. 'A group of beggars at the entrance to the crypt which served Mir as a model for his painting The Cathedral of the Poor.' Courtesy of the Col·legi d'Arquitectes de Catalunya.

200. Photograph taken during construction of the Sagrada Família. 'Photo taken in late afternoon after work had finished for the day.' Courtesy of the Col·legi d'Arquitectes de Catalunya.

201. Rusiñol, Santiago. *Portraits of the anarchists arrested after the attacks on the Teatre del Liceu*, c. 1893.© Arxiu Fotogràfic del Consorci del Patrimoni de Sitges.

202-203. Lombroso, Cesare. *L'homme criminel*, 1887. Plates VII and IX. Paris: Félix Alcan, 1895.

204. 'La Dynamite en Espagne. Explosion d'une bombe au théâtre du Liceo à Barcelone' [Dynamite in Spain. Explosion of a bomb at the Liceu theatre in Barcelona]. *Le Petit Journal*, No. 157, 25 November 1893.

205. 'La Dynamite au Théâtre de Barcelone'. *Le Progrès Illustré*, No. 153, 19 November 1893.

206. 'La Catástrofe del Liceo' [The Liceu catastrophe], *La Ilustración Ibérica*, 18 November 1893.

207. Ribera Cirera, Romà. *Sortida del ball* [Leaving the Ball], c. 1894.
The Liceu held dances for Barcelona's high society, a recurring theme in paintings of the time. © Museu Nacional d'Art de Catalunya, Barcelona.

208. The unexploded Orsini bomb from the Liceu, made by Josep Sabí. Photo: Pep Parer. © MUHBA.

209-210. Illustrations published in *La ilustración ibérica*, op. cit.

211. Gislebertus. Lintel of the north portal of the Cathedral of Saint Lazare in Autun, c. 1130.

212. Gaudí, Antoni. The Rosary Chapel of the Sagrada Família, 1894-1897. Detail of the *Temptation of Man* corbel. Photo: © Pere Vivas /Triangle Postals.

213. Id. The Rosary Chapel with the *Temptation of Man* corbel on the right. *Mediterráneo*, 2 April 1927.

214. Casas, Ramon. *Garrote vil*, 1894. Archivo Fotográfico Museo Nacional Centro de Arte Reina Sofía.

215. The execution of Santiago Salvador, Barcelona, 1894.

216. Casas, Ramon. *Yard of the old Barcelona prison* (The Corders courtyard), c. 1894.
© Museu Nacional d'Art de Catalunya, Barcelona.

217. Dalí, Salvador. *L'Énigme de Guillaume Tell*, 1933.
Photo: Moderna Museet / Stockholm.

218. Lenin in Moscow, anonymous photograph, 21 April 1921.

'Immortal Ruins'

219. Escaler Milà, Lambert. Female bust with mirror, c. 1902.

220. Dalí, Salvador. *The Great Masturbator*, 1929. Archivo Fotográfico Museo Nacional Centro de Arte Reina Sofía.

221. Gaudí's funeral, *Mundo Gráfico*, 16 June 1926.

222. Bataille, Georges. Diagram of *Le jeu lugubre* published in *Documents*, No 7, pp. 297-302, 1929.

223. Le Corbusier, facing pages of *Vers une architecture*. Paris: Crès, 1924 (2nd ed.).

224. Dalí, Salvador. *Monument impérial a la femme-enfant*, 1929. Archivo Fotográfico Museo Nacional Centro de Arte Reina Sofía.

INDEX